ARISTOTLE'S CATEGORIES

and

CONCERNING INTERPRETATION

with

COMMENTARIES

A Global Academic Publishing Book

ARISTOTLE'S CATEGORIES

and

CONCERNING INTERPRETATION

with

COMMENTARIES

Volume I
THE ORGANON

Translation and

Commentary by

Kenneth A. Telford

For information, contact
State University of New York Press, Albany, NY
www.sunypress.edu

ISBN: 1-883058-82-1

Institute of Global Cultural Studies
Binghamton, New York

CATEGORIES

and

CONCERNING INTERPRETATION

with COMMENTARIES

TABLE OF CONTENTS

Introduction   v

Aristotle's Life   xxi

TRANSLATIONS

Categories   1

Concerning Interpretation   39

COMMENTARIES

The Philosophy of Aristotle
        and the Place of Logic   63

Categories   107

Concerning Interpretation   159

INDICES   197

INTRODUCTION

These translations of Plato and Aristotle differ substantially from any prior translation of them because of significant discoveries recently made about both the Greek language, and the procedural assumptions used by these authors. Not only are there now considerable differences in what they literally say, but there are even greater differences in the interpretation that can reasonably be made of what they say. For the text itself, debated for centuries, is now far more secure than ever before, for the procedure controlling it is now understood. Gratuitous textual problems, that resulted from conflicts in procedural assumptions between writer and translator, are now set aside. The understanding of Aristotle's procedure has also occasioned a reëxamination of the function of translation. For British scholarly customs, which dominated American scholarship as well, made untenable assumptions greatly obscuring ancient thought.

Is it, for example, the task of a translator to make a writing over 23 centuries old speak like anything other than what it originally attempted and purported to be? Is nothing lost if a work written about 340 years B.C., be made to sound as if written at the time of the translation? It is better to be 'brought up to date' by speaking in current vernacular? Should the values and concerns of the writer be disguised to look like those of the reader? Should translations cater to readers unwilling even to attempt to understand other cultures? Is it more important that the translation should seem familiar and easy to read than that it clarify what the writer intended? For what point is there to reading another man from another age if one is not willing to understand him as he understood himself, speaking of things as he did?

In the interests of those expert in the topic but not the Greek, should not difficulties in the text be just as evident in the

v

translation as in the original? If the translator has problems understanding the text, is it proper, as is so often done, for him to change the text to suit his guesses as to what the writer ought to be doing, and then keep the reader from knowing either of that change or the reasons for it? And what value are his guesses when most translators are trained only generally in the Greek, and have little or no training in the topic translated? Is his knowledge of Greek, with little or no training in psychology, physics, or philosophy, warrant that a translator has greater skill in understanding these texts than any specialist in these fields not knowing the original tongue? Is such uneducated confidence about the text justification for his destroying both the original facts and the evidence for any change? Is the reader's ignorance of the original language sufficient justification for depriving him of what the text actually says, so that he might decide for himself what it might mean? Isn't it, not simply more honest, but more productive of truth, to make the translation as precise and literal a rendering as possible, and leave problems and guesses to footnotes or separate treatises? Classical linguistic scholars as a group have far greater preference for poetic matters than any of these studies, as is obvious from their selection of terms for abbreviated lexicons. For there the terms used in ancient scientific dispute are mostly removed in favor of the terms of ancient poetry.

If the translator thinks there should be different words where the author uses the same word, is it legitimate to change the word, especially without notifying the reader? Isn't there a legitimate presumption that the author had a reason for repeating the word, so the fact should be available to the reader? If the translator thinks another is needed, shouldn't he first go back and reëxamine the first choice, for another word might be more adequate? It is the Greek use of a word that is the primary evidence for its meaning, not the lexicon which must itself defend its interpretation by going back to Greek use. And lexicons are notorious for giving a torrent of English equivalents, each given as equal to the Greek word, but in fact expressing both more and less than the Greek because adequate only in narrow circumstances. There is a profusion of what is merely possible, inapplicable except in special cases, instead of an extended statement precisely explaining the word's usage. The reason is that most lexicographers think of words sophistically as a matter of substituting counters. But the very fact that in another place another translation is thought necessary, is the sign that the first word chosen fails to convey the full or exact meaning of the Greek.

Most importantly, shouldn't it be the task of the translator to see if the writer has not himself given the clues to his own use of words? Aristotle especially is forever saying 'λέγω,' by way of indicating the meanings of his words, which nearly all translaters then on other occasions blithely ignore. Shouldn't the translator already have observed the range of meaning an author has for a word, when he first translates it?

Is it legitimate to change the syntax and sentence structure because the translator thinks it sounds better or is more efficiently stated in another way? Or should the original structure be kept as closely as the similarity of the two languages makes possible, since the very way in which the words are put together is a great part of the meaning of the original? Should the ways of speaking, peculiar either to the man or his time and place, be put into modern idioms, whether or not they accurately reflect the subtleties of his thinking? And wouldn't this be especially true if some peculiarities appear because he is trying to say something never articulated before? And even if it is true that there are now better ways of saying what he says, shouldn't his formulation be kept so that very evidence for the equivalence is preserved?

These commentaries on Aristotle and Plato were begun in the hope that the reader might read them while using any of the existing translations. But, as said in the commentary on the *Nicomachean Ethics*, in almost every translation of every treatise, as often as not, Aristotle does not make the statement on which one is commenting, or says it with a greatly different meaning. For where there is a puzzle, the translation is often determined more by what the translator has assumed Aristotle should say, than by what in fact he does say. And it is the most crucial issues that are most often effected, for with gratuitous issues no one bothers.

There are in fact two ways in which the thoughts of an author can be corrupted, for there are two functions involved in the handling of old texts, though often both functions are assumed by the same man. There is first the task of the editor who decides from several extant manuscripts, where there are differences between the extant copies, which is the defendable reading. If the sense of the text is affected, one often needs to decide first what the author's philosophic position implies. But this requires far more than knowledge of Greek, It requires knowledge of the author's topic, which is seldom the case, as we said. Then there is the fact that translation itself, putting the same thoughts in another language, clearly involves some interpretation, which again presumes the translator knows, not simply the two languages in a general way, but the precise thoughts and purpose of the writer on this topic. In the performance of either function a scholar may, without any consciousness of his doing so, project upon his text, not the procedural assumptions of the author, but his own, especially when he is not a very conscious person, and oblivious to the peculiarities of his own way of thinking.

For one whose understanding of Plato and Aristotle comes only or mainly through translation, that understanding can be no more precise than the faithfulness of the translation to the original text. It is not simply that minor nuances of the Greek may not be rendered. It is not simply that we are forbidden crucial but incidental information of the man or his times. Rather it is that the whole point of the text is often drastically changed to fit either matters totally accidental to the text, or the preconceptions of the translator concerning the topic of the text. What is more, the translator is usually quite unconscious of this projection.

The medieval translations of William of Moerbeke were punctiliously literal, so that Thomas Acquinas absolved himself of any responsibility to learn Greek and yet had a text with almost every characteristic of the original. If it is Aristotle one wants to understand, Moerbeke's translation is infinitely more accurate than anything more recent. This, of course, is possible only because of the great similarity between Greek and Latin in both their syntactical and semantic structures. Modern English, if only for the fact it lacks the inflectional and syntactical structure of ancient languages, is so different as to make this degree of literalness impossible. And to this must be added every difference between our civilization and theirs, for language in every particular conveys the assumptions, the proclivities and the biases of its times. This is so far from justifying the great tendencies in translations to make ancient texts speak in modern idiom and sound contemporary or adhere to a style not found in the original, that in fact it cries for the reverse. For the thoughts and manners of the ancients are not those of the present, and the terms and manner in which they expressed themselves should never be translated into contemporary idiom, even if, in some rare case, it is true they are the same, else the evidence for that identity is lost. The identity always needs an argument and is never an obvious fact. Yet what was most important to past peoples is almost always what is most peculiar to them and most difficult to put into contemporary idiom. It is also what we should be most concerned with transmitting, though in fact it is what we, in our arrogance, tend to respect the least. If we care for truth, we do not look to the past assuming that it mirrors ourselves.

Many modern scholars with fearsome reputations have scoffed at literal translations. For example, what young teacher would jeopardize his career by incurring the scathing ridicule of Francis M. Cornford whose bombast shows he put the values of the market place over the value of truth. Yet Cornford's ridicule was the projection of his own fears, for his whole plea for pleasantness of style was based on the fear that scholarly accuracy would appear ridiculous. But who would be affronted by a literal translation that appears awkward to modern taste because of the requirements of precision? It would clearly be an affront only to an audience of dilettantes little concerned with truth. There is no way a foreign thought in a foreign tongue can be made to seem familiar in the idiom of a culture centuries removed, without distorting it almost in proportion to its profundity. The effort to 'sweeten the wormwood of philosophy,' even in Lucretius, was for acceptability, not truth. Let Cornford and other sophists have their fear of ridicule. There is nothing liberating in cultural isolation, nothing educational in not looking beyond ourselves.

These translations, therefore, are concerned with one thing and one thing only, to render the thoughts of the ancients in such a fashion as to maximize the ability of the reader to determine every nuance of the original. This means giving the reader the maximum of relevant evidence to find the answers, and not assuming that the translation itself should supply those answers without argument. Translation must separate itself, as much as possible, from interpretation, relegating these matters to footnotes and separate commentaries where they can be honestly identified. It must reproduce as precisely as possible all the nuances of the original, especially by keeping the terminology and structure as consistent as the original. For there is nothing more damaging to the thoughts of a philosopher than the assumption that a different context necessitates a different translation for the same expression. It is falsified by the mere fact that the author used the same term. The problem is solved by making the reader understand the writer's use of his terms, not by constantly hunting for a new word. Perhaps this means the language of the translation is put to new uses, but this happens with any creative thinker, for there is no fact more evident than the creative use of language to express the difference in a man's ideas. The very awkwardness of the translation is a notice for the reader's attention, while changing the translation to suit the context keeps the reader from understanding the true compass of a word.

There can be no understanding of the advantages we claim in the present translation, without examples. There are also some important discoveries in the very nature of the Greek, affecting translation, which are not recognized even in the most auspicious lexicons. Most of our argument concerning the details of translation must, by the nature of the case, be found scattered about in both the translations and the commentaries in their appropriate locations. For out of context, as in this preface, the significance of the difference is often lost. But some words can be discussed in general. The examples we give are few, out of the hundreds which we might have chosen, but illustrate the many inaccuracies that can be observed on virtually every page of every extant translation of the Greek philosophers. There have been only a few translators with enough integrity to refuse the fatuous model set by W. D. Ross in the 20's. For it is to the laxity of Ross's standards that we owe much of the current misdirection in our understanding of Greek philosophy. Jowett lacked observation, precision, and an understanding of procedural differences. But it was Ross who taught translators not only to write in jargon out of touch with the original, but to interfere with the original without revealing the interference.

We will focus mainly on terms that are crucial for logic, and therefore touch any topic. One of the most important distinctions in ancient Greek, though less significant as the centuries pass because modern writers avoid the problem, is the distinction between those phases of intellectual activity that are immediate, or what used to be called intuitive, and those that are mediate or cursive. Three important treatises, the *Metaphysics*, *On the Soul* and the *Posterior Analytics* start their whole procedure with this distinction. It is the difference between faculties dealing with principles and conclusions. Principles are the methodologically primary things assumed by the thinker, with no methodological procedure for establishing them on the basis of something else. Conclusions are grasped as the implications of principle by some methodological procedure. Though Plato and Aristotle differ greatly on what is prior, and how the prior justifies the posterior, they use the same language to convey this priority. For both them, understanding, νοῦς, grasps what is prior, while reason or argument, λόγος grasps what is consequent. But not a single translator has either understood this or followed its implications. In both Plato and Aristotle, and in the fragments of other Greek philosophers, those intellectual activities that constitute an immediate grasp of a content are acts of either understanding, νοῦς, consideration, γνώμη, comprehension, σύνεσις, or judgment, κρίσις. All these faculties Aristotle explicitly distinguishes in the *Nicomachean Ethics*, but no translator takes these distinction seriously, and when the words reappear in other treatises, not only are these distinctions ignored, but their difference from the cursive faculties is also ignored. Yet all these distinctions are fundamental even to the nature of ancient Greek itself.

The cursive intellectual faculties are those which connect and disconnect, in differing ways, the content of the immediate faculties. They are reasoning or arguing or syllogizing, διαλέγω, and συλλογίζομαι, thinking, διανοέομαι, rendering an account, ἀποδίδωμι, etc. This list might be greatly extended. The point is that every Greek philosopher and scientist, not just Aristotle, made this distinction, for it is built into the nature of any procedure of inquiry, and therefore into the Greek language which reproduces the distinction better than English, though nothing in Liddell and Scott informs one of the fact. Principles, whatever the notion of principle in a mode of thought, are grasped by some immediate faculty, understanding, νοῦς, or consideration, γνώμη, or comprehension, σύνεσις, or judgment, κρίσις. But things that are consequent to principles, and have their justification through principles, are grasped by reason, λόγος, or thought, διάνοια, or some other mediating faculty, a faculty that grasps predications between contents, not the contents themselves.

Here and there in translations of the Greeks this distinction is accidentally recognized, but never consistently, which is why in the *Metaphysics* Aristotle is always erroneously quoted as saying god is 'thought thinking on thought.' But what he says is that "understanding understands itself by virtue of grasping [itself]

xii

with the understandable." The word is νοῦς, not διάνοια, but no translation distinguishes them. In the *Nicomachean Ethics*, in contrast, he says that understanding, νοέω, contemplating, θεωρέω, are divine attributes, too 'strong' for man's continued activity, while the function of the human given in the ethics is only reason, λόγος, and thinking, διάνοια. That is why understanding is infallible, you either have it or not, while reasoning can be done in error. Understanding has no dysfunctional alter ego as prudence has cleverness. Obviously translators have not understood that understanding is not thinking. God does not think because the only thing that thinks is the 'sunolon,' the thing of both form and matter. One needs a sense organ in order to think, or even to understand by abstraction from perception, but not to understand as god does, by inner inspection. There are no extant translations of Aristotle in which this distinction can be read, because no translator has understood the difference between the two faculties. Allowing for the differences between their notions of what a principle is and how methodologically it is used, precisely the same distinction is found in Plato and is implicit in the fragments of other ancient Greek scientists and philosophers.

Concerning intellectual functions the lexicons are just as confused as the translators. For example, concerning the relation of ἐννοέω to νοέω, they have not seen that in both Plato and Aristotle, and in Greek generally, the former is the incomplete or primitive stage of the latter. It is ἐννοέω that is used in Book I of the *Metaphysics* by Aristotle to indicate the first growth of the intellectual from perceptible objects, not νοέω which is the mature reflexive activity. It is ἐννοέω that is used by Plato in Book I of the *Republic* to indicate Thrasymachus' potential for intellectual competency, to contrast with what he has actually attained.

The lexicons are also confused about other subtleties which yet must be as exact in the English as in the Greek. For example, Liddell and Scott are confused about inflectional endings like ημα which strictly distinguish the object of a faculty as existing in the organ from the faculty. They say ἐννόημα equals ἔννοια, b difference is the same as that between νόημα and νοῦς, in one case the thing understood, in the other the faculty of understanding, and in each pair the distinction is just as important.

If it is argued that this distinction between immediate and mediate faculties might be true of Aristotle's use of the Greek, because he has fixed first principles, but not of Plato because he has no fixed first principles, then we invite a closer look at Plato. Is there in fact any well known commentator on Plato, whether Cornford, Taylor, etc. who has understood either the function of principle in Plato, or how and where to find his principles? They therefore do not know that Plato makes precisely the linguistic distinction between immediate understanding and mediate reason and thought that Aristotle does, though the use of it is as different as their philosophies. But as long as it is not understood that 'what exists through understanding,' διάνοια, or διά νοῦς, cannot be the understanding itself, νοῦς, but something else, thought or reason, existing on the basis of understanding, or understanding in a vastly different function, both Plato and Aristotle will to that extent be understood erroneously and superficially.

Everyone knows that Aristotle sharply distinguishes 'the fact' or 'the that' in experience, τὸ ὅτι, from 'the why' or 'the because of that,' τὸ διότι. The distinction is basic to the definition of science. But no one sees that when seeing, εἴδω, is distinguished from knowing, γιγνώσκω, it is the difference between immediately given fact, τὸ ὅτι and the why of the fact, τὸ διότι. In ancient Greek, just as we do in common parlance, they said they 'saw the fact' but 'knew the cause.' Even in Plato the distinction is iron-bound, which indicates it should be incorporated into Liddell and Scott. Compare the incidence of both verbs in Plato's dialogues and the occasion and contexts of their use, as in Book I of the *Republic* where, because the dialogue is in its initial and undeveloped stage, εἴδω occurs 23 times and γιγνώσκω only 4. For Socrates and his friends claim only that they 'see,' not that they 'know.' But the distinction is badly confused in Liddell and Scott because of one misunderstood line in Aristotle.

The Greeks even distinguished between merely observing the existence of what happens to be a cause of something else, and observing that it is in fact a cause of that thing, just as we also do. For example we might not only say "I see that you sold that stock today," but we might also say "I see why you sold that stock today." Yet when we want to emphasize our observation of cause in relation to its effect we say "I know darn well why you sold that stock, it was to pressure others to sell theirs." If the text is to be accurately reproduced, the translation must do all that the text does. If the translation operates like an axe while the text acts like a scalpel, the loss can be tremendous. Thus much is lost if the translator thinks Liddell and Scott are correct and εἴδω, like γιγνώσκω, can mean 'to know,' for in truth, as the ancients idiomatically used Greek, it never did. The relation, in fact, is the reverse of what they say under γιγνώσκω, for they misunderstood both what they quote and the verbs' general use.

There are innumerable cases, when the translator has not understood the text and lexicons have not grasped more subtle aspects of Greek, in which distinctions carefully made by Aristotle are simply ignored. At 2a19 and elsewhere Aristotle distinguishes what is predicated 'of' something and what is predicated 'by virtue of' something. Only the second is a necessary or scientific predication, and on this the whole of science rests. The predication that is simply 'of' an underlying object, using the genitive case, is an accidental predication. The very possibility of demonstration depends upon the difference. Yet every translation of Aristotle has totally ignored the distinction and κατηγορεῖσθαι τοῦ ὑποκειμένου has been translated precisely the same as κατηγορεῖσθαι καθ' ὑποκειμένου. And this in spite of the fact that Aristotle himself says that accidents may be predicated 'of' things, but are not predicated 'by virtue of' what underlies them.

The confusion concerning κατά is equally great with its use in καθόλου, for translators have consistently translated this as 'universal,' whereas in fact it means 'by virtue of the whole,' a radically different notion. In this case the confusion is caused by a failure of translators to see the difference between Aristotle's functional conception of logic and modern statistical notions which stem from the sophists of Aristotle's day. Even G. R. G. Mure's use of 'commensurately universal' is equally statistical and did not correct the confusion.

One of the more distressing problems is produced by editors and translators who change the text, simply because they have not understood what the text says, almost always without letting the reader know the text is different than the translation they are given. A peculiarly flagrant case is the *Nicomachean Ethics*, Bywater's change at 1107a1 of ὡς to ᾧ, a trifling change in notation, but enormous in its implications. For by replacing 'as' with 'by that by which' he made Aristotle say morality is not reasoning about practical situations 'as' the prudent man would do it, but simply acting 'by' a rule, the right one, of course, but doing as he was told, not determining it for himself. If was an exceptionally obtuse error, not just because any mature man ought to know better, but because Aristotle had just spent lines 1105a17 - b18 arguing that very point. Till now only one translator of the *Nicomachean Ethics* has been found who has avoided Bywater's misdirection, though that translator was victim to countless others. For most have meekly followed Bywater without a whimper. The *Organon*, the *Metaphysics*, the *Phaedo*, the *Republic*, and just about every other work of Plato and Aristotle contain such redactions based on such ignorance.

Sometimes, even when Greek writers advise the reader, translators simply ignore the matter. For example, Aristotle says there is a great difference between things that are 'different,' διά-φορος, and things that are merely 'other,' ἕτερος or ἄλλος, for two men are 'other,' but do not 'differ' as men, for a difference is a matter of form. Things 'other' are of the same form. Yet every translator translates these words the same. So also δύναμαι, 'to be able,' is translated the same as ἐνδέχομαι, 'to be possible,' though the first means lack of faculty in the thing, the latter any impediment at all, so that the first is a species of the second.

These examples could go on for dozens of pages, but the greatest problem in translations by far is failure to observe the original continued use of a single term, and the contrary lack of judgment, the translation of different terms by the same term, as well as substituting genus for species or species for genus. For example, in the case just cited, in order to secure what they thought Aristotle ought to have meant, the word λόγος, 'argument,' had to be given a meaning it never has for Aristotle, the notion of a 'rule' or guidance for action. A λόγος, or argument, is any predication, an expression, ῥῆμα, said of a name, ὄνομα. For an argument is the statement of reason's grasp of a ratio or proportion between two categorized items of experience. But to translate λόγος as 'rule' or 'definition' or any other specific sort of predication, would be like giving 'monkey' each time the term 'primate' is used. When his writings are examined carefully Aristotle is found never to use 'argument, λόγος, for definition, ὁρισμός, or rule, κανών, or any other of its species. Nor are logical limits semantic, as ὅρος is not simply a term, if term means a part of speech, nor so used by any other Greek author, but refers to bounded existing things, the limits of the analysis of inquiry onto its parts. The confusion caused by this misunderstanding led to a special entry for the term in Liddell and Scott, against the whole Greek history of the word, to accommodate the projection of modern semantic practice upon Aristotle's logic.

Other rather serious confusions of this sort are those between 'appetite,' ἐπιθυμία, and 'desire,' ὄρεξις, between 'anger,' ὀργή, and 'fervor,' θυμός, between 'to prefer,' αἱρέω, and 'to choose,' προαιρέω, many times even in the face of Aristotle's deliberate and explicit distinction between the terms. The translator too often simply takes the first association that pops into his mind, thinking it makes little difference, where a more careful survey of a word's use might reveal something more accurate that will include and exclude the cases it should.

Sometimes, instead of changing the translation of a word because the context has changed, the translator thinks there are a host of Greek terms for which the same English word is quite adequate, and what difference if Aristotle or Plato change their terms. Some times the least association is sufficient to justify the change. Since you can't make choices without purpose or without pursuing some thing, what is wrong with translating προαίρεσις as 'pursuit' or 'purpose,' and in fact if we read Liddell and Scott carefully, they encourage such sloppiness, while Aristotle and Plato, ignored, stand in denial, if only we could read.

But the most egregious collapsing of careful distinctions, in precisely the most difficult works in which precision is most necessary, is the thoroughly careless lumping together, in spite of Aristotle's continual and repeated cautions to the contrary, of the words οὐσία, 'substance,' τὸ τί ἐστι, 'the what it is,' τὸ τὶ ἦν εἶναι, 'the being that was,' and καθ' αὑτό, 'by virtue of itself,' by translating them all as 'essence' or 'essential.' We avoid the word 'essence,' for the only word that linguistically, but not connotatively, could legitimately be so translated is οὐσία, and Aristotle continually indicates, almost presaging our differing use, that 'substance' means not only 'essence,' but the 'sunolon' of form and matter, and even matter alone. This is a consequence of the range of philosophic procedures. In both the *Metaphysics* and the *Posterior Analytics* Aristotle tells his reader that τὸ τὶ ἦν εἶναι, 'the being that was,' is only part of τὸ τί ἐστι, 'the what it is,' yet both are continually translated the same.

But these, along with literally hundreds of other misconceptions, depend on context, and so must mostly wait the appropriate occasion in text or commentary. How much a difference this makes to one's understanding of the Greeks depends upon where one's understanding is. But the difference is hardly small.

And what is given only scratches the surface, as a reading of a literal translation will show. What we would like to emphasize is that there is often an emphasis on precision in ancient thought that is turned casual in the modern mind, sometimes to the point of indifference, perhaps due to our sense of comfort. When man first lifted his head to the extent he could write a text as profound as the Book of J, he was moved, as J himself says, by nothing so much as the things that distinguished him from the other animals. Like so many pendulum movements against the status quo, this insight went beyond its rightful mark, and humanity was accorded a place in existence it did not deserve, denying it was animal.

But that first glimpse into the power of mind was an exhilaration that we with our jaded view of things have lost. The difference explains why inflected languages have been replaced by positional ones, why ten amanuenses copying the dictation of an author before the days of printing could rival modern typesetters for accuracy, so that jumping back eight centuries from the Masoretic texts to the Dead Sea Scrolls discovered that very little variation had been introduced.

For it was our ancestors, not us, who thrilled at the ability of language to be precise. Inflected languages are demanding upon the user, while positional syntax has the laxity that accords with less concern about niceties. Our history abounds with other examples of the same avoidance of precision. It is why prose was posterior to poetry, why sonnets were lost in the push towards free verse. For prose and free verse were not discovered. They were already in use when poets drew our attention to them in the name of their own release from the restriction of self-imposed limitations. For it was the challenge, freely accepted, of restricting poetic forms and rules, that tested one's ingenuity and mettle, which later man gave up as 'not liberating,' for he had come to confuse freedom with license. And our poetry suffers for this. It is easy to confuse pleasure and the lack of constraint with happiness, for freedom is a responsibility and a care.

As long as man was new, had just discovered himself, the urge to use his powers to the full was itself the fullest. It was when he became accustomed to himself that ennui set in, and from enterprise the weight of culture centered more on comfort. Each new culture, each new generation, gives us the resemblance of a new freshness, but the pace of culture from the exploratory and heuristic to the stolid and the comfortable is relentless, as sociologists tell us that early democratic idealism turns to later republican satisfaction with what one has secured. The ancients are profitably read if only to remind us of our more affirmative, even if less sophisticated, selves.

It is a fact worth noting, and quite consonant with our notion above concerning ancient precision, that civilization, before achieving its modern sophistication, showed a marvelous respect for texts, reproducing them with remarkable faithfulness without using subjective standards of authenticity. But modern scholarship, with only a few exceptions, seems to assume it knows better than the ancients of ancient intent, and has stooped to absurd alteration of the facts to make its judgments hold.

A literal translation of Aristotle's text must be regarded as the first order of priority in the attempt to understand him, and a commentary must be suspect that calls for crucial emendations of the original for less than overwhelming reasons. The text as edited by Immanuel Bekker in 1831 has been subject through the years to incredible emendation by many scholars. Almost all this 'correction,' if Aristotle's philosophy is understood, is gratuitous affectation or simply in error, with the text itself as evidence for the error.

This volume will serve as the introduction to the other volumes of Aristotle's *Organon*, and includes in its commentary the place of logic in the philosophy of Aristotle. It is the commentary on the *Metaphysics* that deals with the substantive rather then the procedural aspects of Aristotle's philosophy, his conception of the limits to man's ultimate quest imposed by the nature of what is. The *Organon* is that part of Aristotle's philosophy that gives his conception of the role of the inquirer in respect of that reality. And it is perhaps in this aspect of his philosophy that there is some of the greatest need for rethinking due to the juggling of what he said.

ON ARISTOTLE'S LIFE

It is also appropriate to use this volume which Aristotle's early editors reasonably thought should be first, to set forth some things known of his life, since often extraneous happenings and writings serve to illuminate one another. There is also a legitimate pleasure in associating the events of a thinker's life with the larger themes with which he concerned himself.

Of the three most notable Greek thinkers, including Socrates and Plato, Aristotle is the only one not an Athenian. He was born in 384 B.C. in Stagira, a Greek colonial town on the Macedonian coast of the Aegean Sea. His father was Nicomachus, one time court physician to Amyntas II, the father of Philip of Macedon, thus making Aristotle an hereditary member of the guild of Asclepiads. Stagira had been colonized from Chalcis, Euboea, an Ionian district some 130 miles to the south. It was Chalcis from which Aristotle's mother came and to which he himself retired shortly before his death in 322 B.C.

At the age of 17, in 367 B.C., he went to study at Plato's Academy. Plato at the time was 61 and the Academy had been functioning for 20 years. Aristotle remained there 20 years, progressing from student to seer, no doubt becoming one of the principle teachers. But he left on the death of Plato when the nephew and protégé, Speusippus, was placed in charge of the Academy, quite possibly at his uncle's wish. There is some debate as to whether Aristotle's departure was due to rancor over the selection of the lightly endowed Speusippus, or due to the rise in Athens of Demosthenes' anti-Macedonian party. Certainly his opposition to Plato's procedure was by this time obvious, and no one sympathetic to Plato's thinking would regard the selection of Aristotle as head of the Academy as appropriate to the continuation of Plato's thought. But it was later proved that an anti-Macedonian climate was equally a cause for moving.

With Xenocrates and Neleus, other students of Plato, Aristotle went first to Assus, on the west coast of Anatolia, south of the ruins of Troy, where there was a small group of philosophers, some of them students of Plato. These had received the favor of Hermias, a eunuch and a man successful in business who had been given the title of prince of a small tract by the Persians. Hermias became Aristotle's student and gave him his niece and adopted daughter Pythias in marriage. It does not seem that Aristotle used marriage as an instrument for social advantage. Rather the facts of Aristotle's life, as well as the attitudes discernible from his writings, seem to show, though he was vitally concerned with practical human affairs and their rational governance, he did not seek direct political participation, but followed the more detached life of contemplation, being of service to others if called, but not as concerned as Plato was with affecting those affairs with his own judgments. Theophrastus had come from Lesbos across the small strait to join the group, and after three years persuaded Aristotle, about 344 B.C., to go to Mitylene on the island of Lesbos where Aristotle is reputed to have added marine biological research to his studies.

Two years later, 342 B.C., either through connections with Hermias, or his own heritage, Aristotle was invited to the court of Philip at Pella to teach, principally for the benefit of Philip's son Alexander, then about 14 years of age. Philip died in 336 B.C., but probably by 340, when Alexander was appointed regent for his father, the need for Aristotle had ceased and left him little reason for continuing at Pella.

Aristotle had developed a friendship with Antipater who by 335 was regent in Macedonia and Greece during Alexander's absence on his eastern campaign. Now, with the Academy directed by his friend Xenocrates, he set up his own school at Athens, called the Lyceum, including Theophrastus among its teachers. Aristotle was now 49, and the 12 years that followed were no doubt the period in which his thoughts reached their full articulation, and during which the extant writings were for the most part composed. There is reason to believe that Antipater, and perhaps even Alexander himself, made endowments to the Lyceum.

With the death in 323 B.C. of Alexander, Antipater had been summoned to Babylon, and an anti-Macedonian party arose in Athens that saw Aristotle as contrary to Athenian interests. A charge of impiety was brought against him, as had been brought against Anaxagoras and Protagoras, and as had led to the death of Socrates. Specifically he was accused of creating a private cult in honor to Hermias by erecting a statue to him at Delphi and writing a poem in his praise. But his complete acceptance by Macedonian power is also suspect, in spite of the endowments, for there is reason to suppose Alexander suspected him of complicity in the plot against his life for which Aristotle's nephew Callisthenes was executed. There is also reason to believe that Aristotle did not regard with favor the political ambitions of Alexander or share his vision of larger political hegemonies.

Aristotle retired to his mother's land in Chalcis, only to die in 322 B.C. the next year at age 62. He left a daughter by his first marriage and a son by his second, named Nicomachus after the grandfather. Strabo, 608-9, tells us that Theophrastus sold Aristotle's library to Neleus, the son of Coriscus of Scepsis, who in 347 also had gone to Assus with Aristotle and Xenocrates, to protect those works from the alien influences at the Lyceum of Strato, successor to Theophrastus, for Strato undertook to reconcile the physics of Aristotle with the atomism of Democritus.

At Scepsis in the Troad, Strabo tells us, the library passed down 200 years, neglected, to Apellicon of nearby Teos, until discovered in a cellar during the ravages of the tyrant Sulla, about 80 B.C., who according to Plutarch brought the works to Rome. Tyrannion put them in order, but the first editor of them is said to be Andronicus of Rhodes, 11th head of the Peripatetic School, first century B.C., who, getting copies, edited them much in their present form. Whether or not there had been other copies of these esoteric works, they were not the writings by which Aristotle's thoughts were known and understood till this time. The immediate influence of Plato and Aristotle after their deaths seems to have resulted in a wide difference between mystical and theological speculations following Plato and experts and technicians following Aristotle.

We shall leave the story of the influence of Aristotle's writings to the speculations of others, for the influence between philosophers is moot as long as two conditions prevail. One is confusion about the procedure of thought employed by each philosopher, the second is confusion about the nature and conditions of philosophic influence. These volumes are concerned only with Aristotle's contributions and their feasible interpretation. Though historians like Jaeger leave a contrary impression, the 'influence' of a man is seldom what it seems to be, and is seldom the same as a true continuation of his thoughts.

Much that has been written about Aristotle's works has been concerned with the accidents of his writings rather than what is proper and essential to them. In particular it seems ridiculous to spend great effort in the attempt to discover when and where certain views were developed or committed to words, and who might have said something similar to what he said, if as we intend to show there is much to be done in simply correcting our views of what his philosophy indeed was. In addition, much that is said about his influence is based on a misconception of the nature of influence. We have spoken of this matter in our introduction to the commentary of the *Nicomachean Ethics*.

The works of a good philosopher are profitably read without previous coaching, for he should be assumed able to introduce his own thoughts. If there is need for commentary, it must use the author's text as evidence for any interpretation, not the interpretation as evidence for the text. Unlike Cornford, then, who appears frightened that the reader might have a mind to think for himself, we seek to present Aristotle without our intrusion, and only then ask the meaning of what he has said.

ARISTOTLE'S

CATEGORIES

1. Things are stated 'homonymous' of which only the name 1
is common, but the argument[1] of the substance by virtue of the
name is other, as both human and what is drawn is animal, for
of these only the name is common, but the argument of the
substance by virtue of the name is other. For if one were to
render of these, what is being an animal in each, one would ren- 5
der an argument proper to each.

Things are stated 'synonymous' of which both the name is
common and the argument of the substance by virtue of the
name is the same, as both human and ox is animal, for each of
these is addressed by the common name animal, and the argument of the substance also is the same. For if one were to ren- 10
der an argument for each, what is being an animal in each, one
would render the same argument.

Things are stated 'derivative' which, in differing from something else by its falling,[2] have their address by virtue of the name
[of that from which it falls], as grammarian is stated from the
grammatical, the courageous from courage. 15

2. Of things stated,[3] some are stated by virtue of interweaving, some without interweaving. Things stated by virtue of inter-

---

1. Λόγος is argument or predication, not definition ὁρισμός, or
speech, φάσις. Cf. fn. 13. A category is not a term, but an act of predicating or accusing something of some form of existence. 'Being named
the same,' ὁμώνυμον, 'being named together,' συνώνυμον, and 'being
named beside,' παρώνυμον, are said of things, not terms, since it is not
the naming of names. Terms instead are 'ambiguous,' 'univocal,' etc.
2. Inflection was called a falling away from what is primary.

1

weaving, then, are such as 'human runs,' 'human wins,' things without interweaving, as 'human,' 'ox,' 'runs,' 'wins.'

20 Of things existing[4] some are stated 'by virtue of' something underlying, but exist 'in' nothing underlying, as human is stated by virtue of a certain underlying human, but is 'in' nothing underlying. Some things are 'in' what is underlying, but stated 'by virtue of' nothing underlying. By 'in what is underlying'[5] I state
25 what is attributed to something, not as a part, but as unable to exist separate from that in which it exists, as something grammatical exists 'in' the underlying soul, but is stated 'by virtue of' nothing underlying, and 'something that is white' exists in an underlying body. For every color is 'in' a body, but stated 'by virtue of' nothing underlying.[6]

1b Some things are both stated 'by virtue of,' and exist 'in,' the underlying, as science, while it exists 'in' an underlying soul, it is stated 'by virtue of' the underlying grammatical. Some things are neither in the underlying nor stated by virtue of the underlying,
5 as some human or horse, for nothing of this sort either exists in or is stated by virtue of the underlying. Simply, things indivisible[7] and one in number are stated by virtue of nothing underlying. But nothing prevents some of these from existing in the underlying, for something grammatical exists in the underlying.
10 3. When one thing is predicated[8] by virtue of another as by

3. Τῶν λεγομένων 'things stated,' not the words used to state. Λέγω, focuses on the object, φημί, to say, focuses on the subject.

4. Both τῶν ὄντων, 'things existing,' and τῶν λεγομένων, 'things stated,' are equally things, either (1) as existing, or (2) as stated.

5. What primarily exists is the individual thing. If the form were 'in' any particular body, it could not be attributed to another, for it cannot be 'in' two places at once. Cf. 2a14 ff, fn. 14, and 3a9 ff.

6. The being of 'what is white' is not the being of the body it is in, though its name is stated of the body. Cf. 2a31-34.

7. I.e., as things: when divided they are no longer things, but parts.

8. These verbs must be distinguished, λέγω, to state, κατηγορέω, to predicate, φημί, to say, ἐρῶ, to express, and προσαγορεύω, to address.

2

virtue of what underlies, whatever is stated by virtue of what is predicated is all expressed also by virtue of what underlies, as human is predicated by virtue of some human, and animal by virtue of human. Therefore, animal is also predicated by virtue of some human. For some human is both human and animal. 15

Of things in other genera and not ordered under one another, their differences are also other in form,[9] as of animal and science. For of animals the differences are what has feet, what has wings, what is in water, what is two footed, but none of these belong to science, for science does not differ from science 20 by being two footed. But of genera under one another nothing prevents the differences from being the same. For of genera those above are predicated of the ones under these, so that whatever differences belong to what is predicated will also be differences of the underlying.

4. Of things stated by virtue of no interweaving, each signi- 25 fies either substance, or how much, or what sort, or related to what, or where, or when, or being situated, or possessing, or producing, or suffering.[10] To express this in outline, substance is such as human, horse; 'how much' is two pechus, three pechus; 'what sort' is white, grammatical; 'related to something' is twice, half, greater; 'where' is in the Lyceum, in the market place; 2a 'when' is yesterday, last year; 'being situated' is lying down, sitting; 'possessing' is being shoed, being armed; 'producing' is cutting, setting on fire; 'suffering' is being cut, being set on fire.

Each of these expressions[11] itself, by itself, in no way states 5 either affirming or negating, but by interweaving these with one another affirming and negating arise. For every affirming or negating seems to be either true or false, while things stated by

9. A form, εἶδος, is the structure of the atomic or uncuttable species, as human. A genus, γένος, is any kind at any level of wholeness.

10. Predicatings, (categorizations), except for the first, are stated in Greek by interrogative adjectives, prepositional phrases, or infinitives interpreted as participles, and not by nouns, as in most translations.

11. Thus predicating is most general expression, ῥῆμα. Cf. 16b6.

virtue of no interweaving are neither true or false, as human,
10 white, runs, wins.

5. What is most commandingly, primarily, and mostly stated substance is what is neither stated by virtue of something underlying, nor exists in something underlying, as a certain human or horse. But secondarily stated substances are (1) the forms to
15 which are attributed[12] the things primarily stated substances, both these and (2) the genera of these forms, as (1) a certain human is attributed in form to human, and (2) animal is the genus of the form. Therefore, these are secondarily stated to be substances, such as human and animal.

It is apparent from what has been expressed that it is neces-
20 sary, of things stated by virtue of what is underlying, for both the name and the argument[13] to be predicated of what is underlying, as human is stated by virtue of some underlying human, and the name 'human' is also predicated.[14] For human is predicated by virtue of some human, and the argument of human is predicated
25 by virtue of some human, for some human is also human, so that both the name and the argument are predicated by virtue of what is underlying.

Of things existing in what is underlying, of most neither the name nor the argument is predicated of what is underlying. In
30 some, while nothing prevents the name from being predicated of what is underlying, the argument is unable to be predicated, as what is white, being in an underlying body, is predicated of what is underlying, for a body is stated to be white. But the argument

12. That is, the individual substance, a particular man, is attributed, ὑπάρχω, literally 'begins under,' the form of man, but not 'by virtue of' the form of man. This form is substance in a secondary sense by being a condition of the existence of primary substance, the individual thing.

13. The word is λόγος, argument, not ὁρισμός, definition. Any rational statement, poetic, moral or scientific, is an argument, a reasoned relation between 'limits.' At 4a36 "Someone is sitting" is said to be an argument. At 72a22 he says definition is not even an assertion.

14. Proof that both things and words are 'stated' of things.

4

of what is white is in no way predicated by virtue of the body.

All other things are stated either by virtue of primary substances underlying or by existing in them. This is apparent from 35 particulars taken readily at hand, as animal is predicated by virtue of human, and so by virtue of some human. For if it were predicated by virtue of no certain human, it would not be predicated on the whole by virtue of human. Again, color exists in body, 2b and thus in some body. For if not in some particular, it would not exist in body on the whole. Thus all the others either are stated by virtue of primary underlying substances or exist in these underlying. Therefore, with primary substances not existing, any 5 other is unable to be. For all others either are stated by virtue of these underlying or exist in these underlying. Thus with primary substances not existing, any other is unable to be.[15]

Of secondary substances the form is more substance than genus,[16] for it is nearer primary substance. For if one rendered what primary substance is, he would render what is more acknowledged and more appropriate by rendering form than genus, 10 as he would render what is more acknowledged of a human by rendering human than animal, for while one is more proper to some human, one is more common, and he would render what is more acknowledged of a tree rendering tree than plant.

Moreover, primary substances, because of underlying all the 15 others, and because all others are either predicated by virtue of them or exist in them, are most stated substances. And as the primary substances are related to the others, so form is related to genus, for form underlies the genus. For genera are predicated by 20 virtue of forms, but forms do not turn about to be predicated by virtue of genera. Thus from these things also form is more sub-

15. Scholars spend much time about trivia. Simplicius, fl. c530 AD, expunged these sentences as redundant, and Bekker followed him. L. Minio-Paluello restored this, but subverted other things, like 11b8-17. Scholarship becomes trivial when, in private, unpublished notes, smoothness of style is thought more important than accuracy of statement.

16. Thus forms and genera are existences, not names.

stance than genus.

Of forms themselves, those that are not genera, no one is more substance than another, for no one renders what is more appropriate by virtue of a certain human by rendering human, than by virtue of a certain horse by rendering horse. So also of primary substances, no one is more substance than another, for a certain human is not more substance than a certain ox.

But it is likely that after primary substances, of other things only forms and genera are stated secondary substances. For of things predicated, only these make primary substance evident. For if one were to render what is a certain human, one will render appropriately by rendering either the form or the genus, and will make what is more acknowledged by rendering human than animal. Of other things one might render, as rendering that it is white, or runs, and anything else of this sort, it will be rendered in an alien way. So that in a likely way only these among other things are stated substances.

Moreover, primary substances, because of underlying all others, are more commandingly stated substances. And as primary substances are related to all others, so the forms and genera of primary substances are related to all the remaining, for all the remaining are predicated by virtue of these, for if it is expressed that a certain human is grammatical, it is then expressed both human and animal are grammatical. So also of the others.

By virtue of every substance it is common not to exist in the underlying. For primary substance is neither stated by virtue of the underlying nor exists in the underlying. Of secondary substances it is thus also apparent they are not in the underlying. For human is stated by virtue of some underlying human, but does not exist in the underlying, for human does not exist in a certain human. So also animal is stated by virtue of some underlying human, but does not exist in some underlying human.

Moreover, of things existing in the underlying, while nothing prevents the name at times from being predicated of the underlying, the argument is unable to be predicated. But of secondary substances both argument and name are predicated by virtue of the underlying, for the argument of human and of animal is predicated by virtue of a certain human. Thus substance must 20 not be among things existing in the underlying.

But this is not proper to substance, since even the difference of a substance does not exist in the underlying. For footed and two-footed are stated by virtue of the underlying human, but do not exist in the underlying. For neither two-footed nor footed exists in human. Also the argument of the difference is predicat- 25 ed by virtue of that of which the difference is stated, as, if footed is stated by virtue of human, the argument of footed is also predicated of human, for human is footed. But let it not disturb us that the parts of substances exist in underlying wholes, there- 30 by necessitating us to say that they are not substances, for things existing in the underlying were not stated in a way so as to be attributed to something as parts.[17]

It is attributed to substances and differences that everything from[18] these is stated synonymously. For every predicating from these is predicated either by virtue of things indivisible[19] or by 35 virtue of forms. For there is no predicating of primary substance, for it is stated by virtue of nothing underlying. But of secondary substances, while the form is predicated by virtue of what is indivisible, the genus is predicated by virtue of both the form and what is indivisible. So also the differences are predicated by 3b virtue of both the forms and what are indivisible. Also the primary substances admit the argument of both the forms and the genera, and the form admits the argument of the genus. For as much as is stated by virtue of what is predicated is also ex- 5 pressed by virtue of the underlying. In the same way also both the forms and what are indivisible allow the argument of the differences. But those things are synonymous of which both the

17. 1a25.
18. From, ἀπό, means 'derived from.'
19. Indivisible, ἄτομος, in being, not ἀδιαιρετός, in reason.

7

name is common and the argument the same, so that everything stated from the substances and the differences is stated synonymously.

10   Every substance seems to signify some this. It is therefore indisputable and true that any primary substances signifies some this. For what is made evident[20] is indivisible and one in number. By the schema of the address, in respect of secondary substances similarly, some 'this' appears to be signified whenever human or
15 animal is expressed. But this is not true.[21] Rather what is signified is 'some sort,' for the underlying is not one as primary substance is one, but human and animal are stated by virtue of many. Yet secondary substances do not signify what sort simply, as what is white, for what is white signifies nothing else than
20 what sort. But form and genus determine 'what sort' concerning substance, for they signify what sort of substance. More existing things are made definite by genus than by form, for one who expresses animal embraces more than one who expresses human.

    That there are no contraries to them is also attributed to
25 substances. For what might be the contrary to primary substance, as to a certain human or to a certain animal, for there is nothing contrary. Nor is there a contrary to human or to animal. And this is not proper to substance, but also to many other things, as of how many. For there is no contrary to two pecheis, nor to
30 ten, nor to anything of this sort, even if one says many is contrary to few, or great to small, still when how much is determined no one says there are any contraries.

    Substance seems not to allow more or less. I state not that a substance is not more substance than another substance, for that
35 this is so was expressed.[22] But rather that each substance, being what it is, is not stated more or less, as, if this substance is

20. That to which phenomena give evidence is substance.
21. Aristotle has been accused of deriving his metaphysics from the accident of Greek syntax. He here shows this is not true.
22. 2b37.

8

human, it will not be more or less human, either more or less the same as himself, nor more or less other than another. For one human is not more human than another, in the way that one thing white is more white than another, and what is beautiful more beautiful than another. And the same thing that is white or beautiful is stated more or less white than itself, as the white body is now stated more white than before, and hot is stated more and less hot. But no substance is stated this. For human is not now stated more human than before, nor any other substance. Thus substance does not admit more or less.

What seems most proper to substance, while being the same and one in number, is being receptive of contraries. Of other things than substance none can be brought forward that has this attribute, of being one in number and receptive of contraries. As color, that is one and the same in number, is not white and black, nor is action that is the same and one in number both base and worthy, and so also the other things that are not substance. But substance that is one and the same in number is receptive of contraries, as some human, being one and the same, becomes at one time white and another black, and hot and cold, and base and worthy. But none of the others appear to be of this sort, if one might not object by saying that argument or opinion are of this sort. For the same argument does seem to be both true and false, as, if the argument 'someone is sitting' is true, when the same one has risen, the same argument will be false. So also in respect of opinion, for if one opines truly that someone is sitting, when the same one has risen, he opines falsely, if the same one holds the same opinion.[23]

But though one were to allow this [objection], there yet is a difference in the manner in which this happens. For concerning substances what is receptive in the changing of contraries are the substances themselves, for by becoming cold from hot they

---

23. When the issue is the argument in itself, not the question of stating it, this qualification is not necessary. Cf. 4b10.

change, for they are alienated [from themselves], and black from white, and worthy from base, and in the same way each of the others is receptive of contraries in receiving a change in itself.
35 But argument and opinion while being themselves immovable abide in all things and in every way, and it is by the thing being moved that the contrary arises concerning these matters. For the argument 'someone is sitting' remains the same, and it is by the
4b thing being moved that the argument is now true and now false. So also concerning opinion. Thus it must be in this manner, by virtue of changing itself, that it is proper to substance to be receptive of contraries.

But even if these were allowed, that opinion and argument
5 are receptive of contraries, this is not true. For argument and opinion are stated to be receptive of some contrary, not when they themselves receive them, but when the passion comes to be in something else. For it is by the thing being or not being that
10 the argument is stated true or false, and not by the same argument being receptive of contraries. For simply, neither argument nor opinion is moved by anything, so that as nothing comes to be in themselves, they are not receptive of contraries.

But substance is stated to receive contraries by itself receiv-
15 ing contraries. For it receives sickness and health, whiteness and blackness, and receiving each of such things itself it is stated to receive contraries, so that it is proper to substance, that is the same and one in number, to receive contraries. Let so much be expressed concerning substance.
20 6. Of the 'how much,' some is determined,[24] some is continuous, and some is composed from parts having placement in relation to one another, some from parts not having placement in relation to one another. Determined are, such as number and argument, continuous are line, surface, body, and besides these,
25 time and place. For of the parts of number, none have a common limit in relation to which the parts of the number are

23. Διορίζω means literally 'to make limits through.'

10

joined, as fives are the parts of ten, but five is not joined to five by any common limit, but they are determined, and three and seven are joined in relation to no common limit, nor on the whole may one grasp in respect of number a common limit of 30 parts, but always determined. Thus number is something determined, and in the same way also argument is determined. For it is apparent that argument is 'how much.' For it is measured in syllables that are long and short.[25] I state argument that arises with voice. For none of the parts of this touch together at a 35 common limit, for the syllables do not touch together at a common limit, but each is itself determined by virtue of itself.

But a line is continuous, for it is possible to grasp a com- 5a mon limit, the point, in relation to which the parts of this touch. In respect of surface the common limit is the line. For the parts of a plane touch together in relation to a certain common limit. In the same way also the common limit is grasped of the parts of body, either the line or the surface, in relation to which the 5 parts of body touch.

Time and place are also of this sort. For time now touches together with what has been released and what is to come. Again, place is continuous, for parts of body occupy a certain place and these touch together relative to a certain common lim- 10 it. Therefore the parts of place also, which each of the parts of body occupy, touch together relative to the same limits as those of the parts of the body.[26] Thus place must be continuous, for the parts of this touch together relative to one common limit.

Moreover, 'how much' on one hand is composed from parts 15 having placement relative to one another, and on the other from parts that do not have placement, as the parts of a line have placement relative to one another, for each lies where it does,

25. Differences in length of vowels were the basis of Greek poetic rhythms, supplemented with variations in pitch as in modern Swedish and Chinese, and not stress as in English and European poetry.

26. Thus body gives substance to place, and thus space in general is simply the measure of body, and not an independent reality.

and one might grasp and render to which part each part lies next
20 in a plane and relative to what sort of the remaining parts it is
joined. In the same way also the parts of a plane have a certain
placement, for in the same way one might render what each lies
next to and with what sort of parts it is joined relative to one
another, and so also with the parts of the solid and the parts of
place.

But one would not look upon number as having parts with
25 a certain placement relative to one another, or lying anywhere, or
the sort of parts that are joined with one another. Nor the parts
of time, for none of the parts of time abide, and in what way
does that which does not abide have any placement? Rather they
are stated to have a certain order, this being prior in time, that
30 later.

Similarly in respect of number. By numbering one before
two, and two before three, there is also a certain order, but no
placement to grasp. Argument is the same way, for the parts of
this do not abide, but once expressed it is no longer possible to
35 grasp, so that the parts must not have placement, if they do not
abide. Therefore some are composed of parts having placement,
some from parts not having placement.

Commandingly, only the things expressed are stated 'how
much,' all the others being accidentally 'how much.' For in look-
5b ing at the latter we state other things are 'how much,' as what is
white is stated much by being over much surface, and an action
or a motion is long by existing through much time. For it is not
by virtue of itself that each of these is stated 'how much,' as if
one were to render how much a certain action is he would define
5 it by the time of one year or in some such way as this, and how
much white he would define it rendered by the surface, for as
much as the surface is, so also would the white be said. Thus
only what we have expressed are commandingly and by virtue of
themselves stated how much, and none of the others are stated
by virtue of themselves, but if stated, then they are stated acci-
10 dentally.

12

Moreover, nothing is a contrary to 'how much.' For it is apparent that there is no contrary in respect of things determined, as two arms length or three arms length or contrary to surface or anything of this sort, for of these there is no contrary. One might say that many is the contrary of few or great of small. 15 But none of these is 'how much,' but rather something relative to something. For no one states something is itself by virtue of itself great or small, but only in referring to something else, as a mountain is stated small, a grain large, the latter by being greater than things of similar kind, the former by being less than things of similar genus. The reference is therefore to something else, 20 since if great and small were stated by virtue of itself, the mountain would never be stated small, or the grain large. Again, we say there are many in a village and few in Athens though it has many times as many, and we say there are many in a house and few in a theater though there are many more in the latter. Two 25 arms length and three arms length and each of such signify 'how much,' but great and small do not signify 'how much,' but signify rather a relation to something, for great and small are contemplated in relation to something else. Thus it is apparent that these belong to relations.

Moreover, whether one assumes or does not assume these 30 to be 'how much,' there are contraries to none of these. For how can there be a contrary to something that is not grasped in itself by virtue of itself, but only as it bears on something else? Moreover, if great and small are contraries, it will happen that the same thing admits of contraries simultaneously, and the same things will be contraries to themselves. For it happens simultane- 35 ously that the same thing is great and small, for in relation to one thing it is small and in relation to another thing the same thing is great, so that the same thing happens to be both great and small simultaneously. Thus contraries are simultaneously admitted. But nothing seems to admit contraries simultaneously, 6a as in respect of substance, while it seems to admit of contraries, yet no one is simultaneously sick and healthy, nor white and

13

black simultaneously, nor do any of the others simultaneously
5 admit of contraries. And it happens these are contraries to themselves. For if the great is the contrary of the small, and the same
thing is both great and small simultaneously, the same thing must
be contrary to itself. But the same thing is unable to be the contrary of itself. Therefore, what is great and what is small are not
contraries, nor are what are many and what are few, so that even
10 if one expresses these, not as relative to something, but as what
is how much, none has a contrary.

The contrariety of 'how much' seems most to be attributed
concerning place. For above and below are assumed contraries,
the room at the middle [of the earth] being stated below, because
15 nothing has more distance in relation to the boundaries of the
cosmos than the middle [of the earth].[27] It seems also that in the
definition of other contraries things are imputed from matters of
place, for things having the most distance from one another in
this genus are defined contraries.

'What is how much' does not seem to admit more and less,
20 as two arms length. For it is not possible for one 'two arms
length' to be more than another 'two arms length.' Nor in respect of numbers, as no three is more three than a five is a five,
nor one three than other threes. Nor is there any time that is
more time than another time. Nor generally of the things expressed is there any one that is stated more or less. Thus 'what is
25 how much' does not admit of what is more or less.

What is most proper to 'what is how much' is that it is stated both equal and unequal. For each 'how much' expressed is
stated both equal and unequal, as body is stated equal and unequal, and number also is stated equal and unequal, and time also
is stated equal and unequal, and in the same way also in respect

27. *On the Heavens*, 268b21, says taking a circle as the whole, the
most distant point is the center or middle. Whether the earth was
viewed as flat or spherical, the rotation of the heavens itself stipulated
the notion of a middle.

of other things expressed, each is stated both equal and unequal. 30
Of the remaining [predicatings] that are not 'how much,' none it
seems is stated equal and unequal, as no disposition is stated
both equal and unequal, but rather similar, and white is never
stated both equal and unequal, but similar. Thus what is most
proper of 'what is how much' is that it is stated both equal and
not equal. 35

7. The sorts of things stated to be 'relative to something' are
those we state exist in reference to^{28} something else or are in
anyway related to something else, as what is greater is stated
what exists in reference to something else, for it is stated greater
than something else. And what is double is stated what exists in
reference to something else, for it is stated the double of some- 6b
thing else. And so also with other things of this sort. What is
relative to something are also such things as habit, disposition,
perception, science, placement. For all the things expressed are
stated in reference to something else, and in no other way. For a
habit is stated a habit (a having) of something, science is science 5
of something, placement is placement of something, and so with
the others. What is relative to something, therefore, is whatever
is stated in reference to something else or in whatever way relative to something else, as a mountain is stated to be great in relation to another mountain, for the mountain is great in relation to
something, and what is stated similar is similar to something, and
so with other things of this sort that are stated relative to some- 10
thing. Lying down, and standing and sitting are certain placements, and placement is among things relative to something.^{29}
But to be lying down and standing and sitting are not themselves
placements but are stated derivatively from the placements expressed.^{30}

28. 'In reference to' is in Greek simply the genitive case, 'of.'
29. Placement, θεσις, always refers to other objects in terms of
which it is placed, and thus improperly translated 'attitude' or 'position.'
30. The situation, expressed by the verb 'to be lying down,' ἀνα-
κεκλίσθαι, is derived from the relative noun 'lying down,' ἀνακλισις.

15

15   Contrariety is attributed also of things relative to something, as virtue is the contrary of vice, each of these being relative to something, and science is the contrary of ignorance. But a contrary is not attributed to everything relative to something, for double has no contrary, nor does triple, nor do others of this
20 sort. And it also seems that things relative to something admit to being what is more and what is less, for what is similar is stated to be more and less, and what is unequal is more and less, each of these being relative to something. For the similar is stated as similar to something, and the unequal as unequal to something.
25 But not everything relative to something admits of more and less. For what is double is not stated to be more or less double, nor is anything of this sort.

Everything relative to something is stated relative to what turns about, as slave is stated slave of the master and master is
30 stated master of the slave, the double is double the half and the half is half of the double, and the greater is greater than the less and the less is less than the greater, and so with others. Except that some differ in the falling by virtue of the diction, as science is stated science of that of which one is able to have science,[31] and that of which one is able to have science is that of which
35 one is able to have science through science, and perception is perception of the perceptible and the perceptible is perceptible through perception. But some do not seem to turn about, if he who renders makes a mistake by rendering what is stated inappropriately, as if one renders a wing in reference to a bird, for it does not turn about that a bird is stated in reference to a wing. For the primary thing of which wing is appropriately rendered is
7a not bird,[32] for it is not of this as bird that wing is stated, but of bird as winged. For many other things are winged that are not

31. An inflectional ending was called a 'falling.' As here, modern languages often need lengthy expression for a simple Greek inflection.
32. One must attribute the difference to that existing by virtue of a whole, or the first in the order from most general, not to simply a species of that whole. Cf. 73b32.

birds, so that if one were to render appropriately it would also turn about, as the wing is the wing of what is winged and what 5 is winged is winged by its wing.

But sometimes it is perhaps necessary to make up names, if there is no name laid down that is appropriate to what is rendered, as if one renders rudder in reference to a boat, the rendering is not appropriate. For rudder is not stated of boat as boat, for there are boats of which there are no rudders. On this ac- 10 count the relation does not turn about, for the boat is not stated the boat of the rudder. But perhaps the rendering would be more appropriate if it were rendered as the rudder is the rudder of the ruddered, or in some such way, for there is no name laid down, and at least the relation turns about, for it has been rendered appropriately, for the ruddered is ruddered to the rudder. And so with other things, as a head is rendered more appropri- 15 ately in reference to what is headed than in reference to animal, for it is not as an animal that he has a head, for many animals do not have a head.

In this way one might perhaps more easily grasp that to which something is related, when no name is laid down, if from the first things [having a name] we assume names also for those 20 things that are turned about in relation to the former, as in respect of the previously expressed, from rudder we assumed what is ruddered. Therefore, everything related to something, if appropriately rendered, is stated in relation to things that are turned about. Since if it is rendered in relation to any chance thing, and not in relation to the same thing that is stated, it will not turn 25 about. I state that there will be no turn about, even with agreed upon relations turned about, and names laid down for them, if it is rendered in relation to some accident and not relative to that which is stated, as if slave is not rendered in reference to master but to human or two footed or anything of this sort, it will not 30 turn about. For the rendering is not appropriate. Moreover, if something is rendered appropriately as related to what was stated, all the other accidental things being stripped off, and only this by

which it was appropriately rendered being left, what is related to
35 this will always be expressed, as if slave is stated in relation to
master, while all the accidents of master are stripped off, as two-
footed, receptive of science, human, and only being master is
left, the slave will always be expressed in relation to this, for the
7b slave is stated the slave of the master. But if what is stated is
ever in relation to what is inappropriately rendered, and the others are stripped off and only that which renders the relation is
left, what is relative to this will not be expressed. For let slave be
rendered as belonging to human and wing belong to bird, and let
5 being master be stripped off human, slave will no longer be expressed in relation to human, for as no longer belonging to
master neither is he any longer a slave. So also if being winged is
stripped off bird, for what is winged will no longer be what is
related to something, for not belonging to a winged thing, wing
10 will not belong to anything. Thus what is stated relative to something needs to be rendered appropriately. And if a name has
been laid down, the rendering will be easy, but if there is none
perhaps it is necessary to make up a name. In this way of rendering, it appears that everything expressed in relation to something
is turned about.

15   Things related to something seem by nature to exist simultaneously, and this is true of most things. For both double and
half exist simultaneously, and double exists in reference to half,
and master exists in reference to slave. And similarly in other
cases. These also are taken together with one another, for there
20 being no double, there is no half, and there being no half there is
no double. In the same way also with other things of this sort.

     But of everything related to something it does not seem true
that it exists by nature simultaneously. For that of which one is
able to have science[33] would seem to exist before the science.
25 For we grasp sciences for the most part of things that are previ-

     33. Not 'what is known,' but 'what is knowable,' for potentiality is
not actuality. Otherwise the point two sentences later is meaningless.

ously present. For there are few or no sciences seen to arise simultaneously with that of which one is able to have science. Moreover, while confuting that of which one is able to have science confutes the science with it, confuting the science does not confute with it that of which one is able to have science. For of what one is not able to have science there is no science, for of nothing there is no longer science. But of the science that does not exists nothing prevents there being that of which there is able to be science, as the squaring of the circle, if at least there is that of which one is able to have science, for while there is no science of this, this is that of which one is able to have science. Moreover, if animals are confuted, the science does not exist, but many things of which one is able to have science are possible. 30

Similarly of perceptual things. For the thing that is percepti- 35 ble seems to exist before the perception, for confuting the perceptible together confutes the perception, but confuting the perception does not confute together the perceptible. For perception concerns body and exists in a body, and if the perceptible is confuted the body is confuted together. For the body is some- 8a thing perceptible, and if the body does not exist then the perception also is confuted, so that the perceptible and the perception are confuted together. But if perception is confuted, the perceptible is not. For if the animal is confuted, while the perception is confuted, there will still be perceptibles, as body, heat, sweetness, 5 bitterness, and all the other perceptibles. Moreover, perception arises simultaneously with the perceptible, for the animal and the perception arise simultaneously. But indeed the perceptible exists before the perception, for fire and water and such things, from which animals are composed, exist also before the animal general- 10 ly is, or the perception, so that the perceptible seems to exist before the perception.

There is a problem whether, as it seems, no substance is stated relative to something, or whether this is possible by virtue of some secondary substances. For in respect of primary sub- 15 stances it is true [that they are not]. For neither wholes nor parts

19

are stated in relation to something, for a certain human is not stated some human of something, nor is a certain ox stated some ox of something. In the same way also in respect of the parts, for a certain hand is not stated some hand of something, but the
20 hand of something, and a certain head is not some head of something, but the head of something. So also in respect of secondary substances, at least most of them, as human is not stated the human of something, nor is ox stated the ox of something, nor is wood stated the wood of something, but is stated the possession of someone.

25 It is apparent therefore that while in respect of such things substance is not what is relative to something, concerning some secondary substances there is a dispute, as a head is stated the head of someone, and a hand is stated the hand of someone, and each of such things, so that these things seem to be relative to something. Therefore, if the definition of things relative to something is adequately rendered, whether no substance is stated of
30 what is relative to something is either quite difficult or unable to be solved. Yet if it is not adequately rendered, but what is relative to something is the same in being as that which is in any way relative to something, perhaps something might be expressed related to this problem.

While the definition rendered before is closely consequent to all that is relative to something, still it is not this, what is itself
35 relative to things, by being stated of other things. From these things it is evident that if one sees something definitely that is relative to something, he also sees that definitely in relation to which the thing is stated to exist. It is apparent, therefore, even from the thing itself. For if one sees a certain this that is among things relative to something, and its being relative to something
8b is the same as having in some way a relation to something, he sees also that to which this is in some way related. For in general if he did not see that to which this was in some way related, he would not see that this was in some way a relation. This is evident from particulars of this sort, as if one sees determinately

that this thing is double, he also straightaway determinately sees 5
that of which it is double. For if there is nothing determined of
which he sees this is double, neither in general does he see that
this is double. In the same way also if he sees that this is more
beautiful, it is necessary also that he determinately sees the things
because of which this is more beautiful. He will not indefinitely 10
see that this is less beautiful, for something of this sort becomes
conviction, not science. For not seeing accurately that this is less
beautiful, if it chances in this way, it is not possible to see that
this is worse than that. Thus it is apparent that it is necessary,
that anyone who sees that something definitely is relative to
something, also sees definitely that to which it is stated relative. 15

But while at least head and hand and each of such things
that are possible of being definably seen are themselves substances, it is not necessary to state that to which they are relative.
For whose head or whose hand it is not possible to see definitely. So that these things might not belong to things relative to
something. But if they are not things relative to something, it 20
would be true to state that no substance is relative to something.
But perhaps it is difficult to declare vehemently about things of
this sort while one has not often investigated them, but it is not
unuseful to raise problems about the particulars.

8. Qualities[34] I state are that by virtue of which we state of 25
what sort some people are. Quality belongs to things stated in
many ways. One form of quality, then, let us state to be habit
and disposition. Habit differs from disposition in being more
stable and more lasting. Of this sort are the sciences and the
virtues. For science seems more stable and more difficult to 30

34. This is the first predicating defined as attributing, not to substances generally, but to human in particular. This is because the being
of the full range of this predicating depends on the completeness of
being of the substance of which it is predicated. Human is the only
substance that admits the full range of possible qualities. Also, as 'of
what sort,' ποῖος, is related to 'quality,' ποιότης, so 'how much,' πόσος,
is related to 'quantity,' ποσότης, cf. *Metaphysics*, V, 1020b2.

21

move, even if one grasps science moderately, if no great change comes about through sickness or something else of this sort, and so also virtue, as justice and temperance and each of such things 35 seem not easily moved or easily changed.

Disposition is stated with things easier to move and quickly changed, as heat and coldness, illness and health, and others of this sort. For a human is disposed in a way by virtue of these, but quickly changes from hot becoming cold and from healthy 9a becoming sick. So also in respect of the others, unless one of these happens itself through an amount of time, by becoming blown up, to be incurable or quite difficult to move, when perhaps one ought to address it as a habit.

It is apparent that people wish to state habits are those that 5 are longer lasting and more difficult to move. For those who do not quite hold on to science and are easily moved, are not said to have the habit, but are at least disposed in a way to science, either worse or better. So that habit differs from disposition by the latter being easily moved and the former longer lasting and 10 more difficult to move. Habits, then, are also dispositions, but dispositions are not necessarily habits. For those who have habits are also disposed in a way by virtue of these things, but those who are disposed do not always have a habit.

Another genus of quality is that by virtue of which we state 15 one is able to box or run, or is healthy or sickly, and simply those that are stated by virtue of a natural power or lack of power. For such things are not stated of each person through his being disposed in a way, but by having a natural power of producing something easily or not suffering anything, as those able 20 to box or run are not stated as disposed in a way, but as having a natural power to do something easily, and are stated healthy as having a natural power to suffer no chance thing easily, and are stated sickly by having a lack of power for suffering nothing. Similarly with those having toughness and softness. For tough- 25 ness is stated of one who has the power of not easily falling apart,[35] softness in having the lack of power for the same thing.

22

A third genus of quality are the affective qualities and passions. These are such as sweetness, bitterness, sourness and all those akin to these, moreover heat, cold, whiteness, and black- 30 ness. It is apparent, then, that these are qualities, for the things receiving these things are stated to be of this sort by virtue of these, as honey is stated to receive sweetness being sweet, and body is white by receiving whiteness. So also in respect of having others. Affective qualities are not stated of things in the sense 35 that the things that receive these qualities are in some way affected. For neither is honey stated sweet by being affected in some 9b way, nor are other things of this sort in any way affected. Similarly heat and coldness are called affective qualities not by the things receiving them being affected in some way, but are each stated affective qualities by being productive, through perception, 5 of a suffering (affection) of the expressed qualities. For sweetness is a certain passion produced in us[36] by virtue of taste, and heat by virtue of touch, and similarly with the others. Whiteness and blackness and the other colors are not stated affective qualities in the manner expressed, but by themselves arising through passion. 10 It is evident that many changes of color arise through passion, for when one is ashamed one becomes flushed, and when in fear, pale, and each of such things. Thus also if one is by nature of the sort to suffer certain passions, it is likely one has himself a 15 similar color, for what was now a disposition in being disgraced becomes a quality of the body, and what was a disposition becomes a natural composition, so that a similar color comes to be by nature.

Therefore, those things that have befallen one, though grasped at the beginning from passions that are difficult to move 20 and steadfast, are stated qualities. For sallowness or darkness [of

35. Lit., 'being divided.'
36. Ἐμποιέω, 'to produce in.' This shows why all qualities are stated in terms of the human being receptive of them. For us to receive something as a passion, the object must have a corresponding quality.

23

skin] arising in standings together by virtue of nature are stated
25 qualities. For we are stated of what sort by virtue of them. Then
sallowness or darkness that happen through lengthy sickness or
sunburn, and are not easily restored or even abiding through life,
are also stated qualities. For in the same way we are stated of
what sort by virtue of these.

But those that are easily broken up and become quickly
30 restored are stated passions. For we are not stated of what sort
by virtue of these. For he who blushes because of being shamed
is not stated a blusher, nor is he who is sallow because of being
in fear stated sallow, but rather one who has been affected. Thus
passions are stated things of this sort, but these things are not
qualities.

35   In the same way we speak of affective qualities and passions
of the soul. For those things that arise straightaway at birth from
10a certain passions are stated qualities, as the manic quality, ecstasy,
anger and such things, for people are stated of what sort by virtue of these, as angry or manic. Similarly those ecstasies[37] that
are not natural, but come to be from certain other things that
5 befall one, are difficult to escape from or even on the whole
immovable, are stated qualities, and things of this sort. For we
are stated of what sort by virtue of these. But those that are
quickly restored are called passions, as if one were more angered
when being pained. For one is not stated prone to anger when
one is more angry in a passion of this sort, but rather one who
10 has been affected. Thus these sorts of things are stated passions,
but are not stated qualities.

A fourth genus of quality is both the figure and shape that
is attributed of something, and moreover in addition to these
straightness and curvedness and anything similar to these, for by
virtue of each of these something is stated of what sort. By being
15 triangular or quadrangular a thing is stated of what sort, and by
being straight or curved. And each thing is stated of what sort by

37. Lit., 'standing outside of one's place.'

24

virtue of its shape. The rare and the dense, the rough and the smooth, seem to signify what sort, but it is likely that things of this sort are alien to dividings concerning quality. For it appears 20 rather that a certain placement of the parts makes each of these evident. For something is dense by its parts being close to one another, rare by being removed from one another, smooth by the parts lying in some way straight, rough by parts being excessive and deficient. Perhaps, then, there may appear to be qualities in 25 another manner, but those which we mostly state are nearly so many.

The things expressed, therefore, are qualities, while things existing by virtue of these are stated what sort derivatively, or stated in some other way than these. Therefore, they are stated as most or nearly all things stated derivatively, as what is white is 30 from whiteness, grammatical from the art of grammar, the just from justice, and in the same way others. But of some, because the quality has no name laid down, it is not possible for these things to be stated derivatively, as he who has the aptitude to run 35 or to box, stated by virtue of a natural power, is stated deriva- 10b tively from no quality, for there is no name laid down for those powers by virtue of which we are stated of what sort,[38] just as there is no name for the sciences also by virtue of which men are stated to have the aptitude for boxing or wrestling by virtue of a disposition. For the science is stated to involve boxing and wrestling, and those disposed are stated of what sort by being 5 derivatively named from these.

But sometimes while there is even a name laid down, what is stated by virtue of what sort is not stated derivatively, as the worthy one is from the virtue, for he is stated worthy by having virtue, but not derivatively from the virtue. But there are not 10

38. ὁ δρομικός is linguistically derived from ὁ δρόμος, 'race course,' and means 'one able to run a race course.' Aristotle's point is that there is no word for the primary reality, the natural ability, to indicate the derivation of the familiar term for the one who has that ability.

many of this sort. Therefore, those things are stated of what sort derivatively from the stated expressed qualities or in any other way from them.

Contrariety also is attributed by virtue of what sort, as justice is contrary to injustice, whiteness to blackness, and others 15 also, and also the things which by virtue of these we state are what sort, as the unjust is contrary to the just, the white to the black. But not all of these are such. For to red, yellow and such colors there are no contraries though they are what sort. Moreover, if one of two contraries is what sort, the remaining one is 20 also. This is evident from the other predicatings taken readily at hand, as, if justice is the contrary of injustice, and justice is what sort, then injustice is also what sort. For none of the other predicatings suits injustice, neither how much, nor relative to something, nor when, nor on the whole any of the others of this sort 25 except what sort. In the same way also with other contraries by virtue of what sort.

Things what sort also admit of what is more or less. For one thing is stated more or less white than another, and more just than another. And it may be the same surface that one 30 grasps. For being white it is possible of becoming yet more white. Not all, but most of them. For if justice is stated more justice, there is a certain problem, and similarly with other dispositions. For some dispute about these sorts of things, for they declare that while justice is altogether not stated more or less 35 than justice, nor health than health, they declare some people 11a have less health than others, and some less justice than others, and similarly with grammatical science and other dispositions. But things stated by virtue of these, indisputably admit of what is more and less. For one person is stated more grammatical than 5 another, and more just and more healthy, and with other things also. But triangular and quadrangular do not seem to admit what is more, nor any of the other figures. For the things admitting the argument of triangle or circle are all triangles and circles in the same way, while those not admitting the argument are none

expressed this more one than another, for a quadrangle is not 10
more a circle than is a rectangle, for the argument for a circle is
admitted by neither. Simply, then, if the argument of what is
proposed is not admitted of both, it is not expressed of one
more than another one. Therefore, not all things of a sort admit
of what is more and less. 15

While none of the things expressed are proper to quality,
similar and dissimilar are stated only of qualities. For one thing is
similar to another thing by virtue of nothing but what sort it is.
Thus the similar or the dissimilar stated by virtue of itself is
proper to quality. 20

One ought not be disturbed if someone declares that having
made a proposal about quality we have accounted together with
it many things relative to something. For habits and dispositions
are relative to something. For the genera of nearly all such are
stated relative to something, but none of the particulars. For 25
science, being a genus, is itself stated relative to something else,
for science is stated of something, but particular sciences are not
stated relative to something else, as grammatical science is not
stated grammatical of something, nor musical science musical of
something, but if these are stated relative to something it is by
virtue of the genus, as grammatical science is stated to be the 30
science of something, but not grammatical of something, and
musical science is science of something, but not musical of
something, so that particular sciences are not relative to something.

We state then that we are what sort by possessing particular
sciences, for these also we possess. For we state men to be having science by having certain particular sciences, so that the par- 35
ticular sciences themselves are qualities, by virtue of which at
times we are stated what sort, and these are not relative to something. Moreover, if it happens that the same thing is both what
sort and relative to something, there is nothing out of place in
counting one thing in both genera. 11b

9. Producing and suffering also admit of contrarieties and

27

what is more and what is less. For heating is the contrary of cooling and being heated of being cooled and being pleased of
5 being pained, so that they admit contrarieties. And they admit more and less, for it is possible to heat more and less, and be heated more and less, as well as to be more or less pained. Therefore, producing and suffering admit more and less.

10 Of these, then, so much is stated. 'Being situated' was expressed in our argument on 'relative to something,' that they are stated derivatively from placements. Of the remaining, 'when' and 'where' and 'possessing,' because they are quite apparent, we state no more than what was expressed at the beginning, that 'possessing' signifies being shoed, being armed, that 'where' is as
15 in the Lyceum, and the others as we expressed about these.

10. Therefore, the things expressed concerning the proposed genera [of predicatings] are adequate. But one must next express,[39] of opposites, in how many ways we are accustomed to place things against one another.

One thing is stated opposed to another thing in four ways, either as relative to something, or as contraries, or as privation and habit,[40] or as affirming and negating. To express this in out-
20 line, each of such things is opposed, as relative to something, such as double to half, as contraries, such as evil to good, as by virtue of privation and habit, such as blindness and sight, as affirming and negating, such as one who is seated to one who is not seated.

25 Those things, then, opposed as themselves relative to some-

39. What follows has been falsely held as spurious. Because an ancient editor gave the treatise this name, does not mean that everything not accounted for by that name is spurious. The subject-matter is simples, not predicatings. See commentary.

40. Ἕξις, 'habit,' (e.g. a virtue is a habit, 1106b36.) derived from the verb 'to have:' not a simple state, but a way of doing. One case in which English verbally distinguishes between the participle (Greek infinitive) and the derivative noun. A habit is a quality, distinguished from the predicating 'possession,' τὸ ἔχειν, both from the same verb.

thing, are stated opposed, or whatever way, relative to them, as the double is related to the half of which it is stated the double. Science as relative to that of which there is able to be science is opposed to it, and science itself is stated what indeed belongs to that of which there is able to be science, and that of which there is able to be science is itself stated relative to the science opposed, for that of which there is able to be science is stated that of which there is able to be science by some science.

Things opposed as relative to something are then themselves stated opposed, or in whatever way, relative to one another. But things opposed as contraries, are themselves in no way stated relative to one another, but are stated contrary one of the other. For the good is not stated the good of the bad, but the contrary of the bad, nor is white the white of the black, but the contrary of the black. Thus these [two] antitheses differ from one another. But those contraries that are such that in those things in which they naturally arise, or of which they are necessarily predicated, either one or the other of these is attributed, these contraries have no middle, while those to which it is not necessary that one or the other be attributed, these always have a middle between. As sickness and health naturally arise in the body of an animal, and it is necessary that either sickness or health be attributed to the body of an animal. Odd and even also are predicated of number, and it is necessary that either odd or even be attributed to number. And there is no middle between these, either sick and healthy, or odd and even.

But those things of which it is not necessary that either one or the other be attributed, of these there is a middle, as black and white naturally arise in body, and it is not necessary that one or the other be attributed to body, for it is not the case that every body is either white or black. And base and worthy are predicated both by virtue of human and many other things, and it is not necessary that either one or the other of these be attributed to that of which they are predicted. For it is not the case that everything is either base or worthy. Some of these are in the middle, as gray is in the middle between white and black, and sallow and other colors, and between base and worthy is what is neither base nor worthy.

For some things names have been laid down for the middle, as the middle of white and black is grey and sallow. But for some there is no easy way to render a middle, but by negating each of the extremes one defines the middle, as what is neither good nor evil and neither just nor unjust.

Privation and habit[41] are stated of the same thing, as sight and blindness of the eye. To express this by virtue of a whole, each of them is stated of that in which the habit naturally arises. We state each thing receptive of a habit is deprived, whenever the thing to which the habit is naturally attributed and when it is naturally attributed, is in no way attributed. For we state the toothless, not what does not have teeth, and the blind not what is without sight, but what does not have it when it naturally has it . For from their genesis some have neither sight nor teeth, but are not stated toothless or blind. Being deprived and having a habit, then, is not privation and habit. For while sight is habit and blindness is privation, possessing sight is not sight, nor is being blind blindness. For blindness is a certain privation, but being blind is being deprived, not a privation. Moreover, if blindness were the same as being blind, they would both be predicated by virtue of the same thing. But while a human is stated blind, human in no way is stated blindness. And these seem to be opposed, being deprived and possessing a habit, as are privation and habit. For the manner of their antithesis is the same. For as blindness is opposed to sight, so also is being blind opposed to possessing sight. And what falls under affirming and negating is not the same as affirming and negating. Affirming is affirmative argument and negating is negative argument, but what falls under affirming or negating is not argument. Yet these are

41. A habit is the having or possessing of something, often transforming the function, as in the case of moral or intellectual habits.

also stated opposed to one another as are the affirming and negating. For the manner of antithesis in these is also the same. For as affirming is opposed to negating, such as 'he sits' and 'he does not sit,' so also is the thing falling under each proposition opposed, namely, 'the sitting' and 'the not sitting.'[42]

It is apparent that privation and habit are not opposed as things relative to something. For what a thing is itself is not stated in reference to something opposed, for sight is not sight of blindness, nor in any other way stated relative to something. In the same way blindness is not stated the blindness of sight, but blindness is stated the privation of sight, and not stated the blindness of sight. Moreover, things relative to something are all stated relative to things that turn about, so that blindness also, if it were relative to something, would turn about with that in relation to which it was stated. But it does not turn about, for sight is not the sight of blindness.

That things stated by virtue of privation and habit are not opposed as contraries is evident from the following. For of contraries of which there is no middle, it is necessary that one or the other be always attributed to the things in which they naturally arise or of which they are naturally predicated. For of those for which there is no middle it was shown that necessarily one or the other is attributed, as in respect of sickness and health, odd and even. Of those for which there is a middle, it is not necessary that one or the other be attributed in every case. For it is not necessary that what is receptive of them be in every case either white or black, nor hot or cold, for nothing prevents something in the middle from being attributed.

Moreover, of those which have a middle it is not necessary that one or the other be attributed to that which is receptive, if

42. This is said in a way opposite to what might be supposed. for the 'thing,' πρᾶγμα, which falls 'under' the predicating, what underlies, is not the human, but 'the sitting' of which the form of human is predicated, as in "the sitting thing is he."

31

one is by nature not attributed of it, as being hot is attributed to fire and being white is to snow, and in respect of these it is
40 necessary that one be determinately attributed, and not either one by chance. For it is not possible for fire to be cold or snow
13a black. Thus it is not necessary in every case that one or the other be attributed to what is receptive, but only the one which by nature is attributed, and to these things determinately one and not whatever chances.

But in respect of privation and habit neither of the things
5 expressed are true. For it is not necessary that one or the other always be attributed to what is receptive. For what does not yet naturally possess sight is stated neither blind nor having sight, so that these must not belong to the sort of contraries which have no middle, nor to those that have a middle, for it is sometimes necessary in all of these that either one or the other be attributed
10 to them. For when the time arrives that it naturally possesses sight, then it will be expressed either that it is blind or that it possesses sight, and not determinately either one, but whichever chances. For it is not necessary either that it be blind or possess sight, but either one that chances. But in respect of contraries which have a middle, it is not necessary in every case that one or
15 the other be attributed, but in some cases what is one is determinately attributed to it. Thus it is evident that things opposed in respect of privation and habit are opposed in neither of the two manners in which contraries are opposed.

Moreover, in respect of contraries, while attributed of what is receptive, changes are able to arise from one to the other, if
20 one is not by nature attributed to something, as being hot is attributed to fire. For what is healthy is able to be sick and what is white to become black and cold hot, and from the worthy the base is able to arise and from the base the worthy. For the base person, being led to a better passing of time and argument,
25 might improve even a little to being better, and if he once grasps a small improvement, it is apparent that it is possible that he change completely or grasp a very great improvement. For always

32

one comes to be more easily moved to virtue, even though grasping a small improvement at the beginning, so that it is likely he will grasp more improvement. And this always arising, he will 30 be completely restored to the contrary habit, if time does not work against it. But in respect of privations and habits, change is unable to arise from one to another, for the change comes from the habit to the privation, but the change from the privation to the habit is unable to come about. For one who is blind does 35 not come again to see, nor the bald become hairy, nor the toothless grow teeth.

It is apparent that what are opposed as affirming and negat- 13b ing are opposed in none of the manners expressed. For only in these is it necessary always that one be true and the other false. For it is not necessary in contraries that one always be true and 5 the other false, nor in relations, nor in habits and privations, as health and sickness are contraries, and neither one is [necessarily] either true or false, and in the same way double and half are opposed as relations, and neither of these is either true or false, nor things by virtue of privation and habit, as sight and blind- 10 ness. And on the whole things not stated by virtue of an interweaving are not either true or false, and everything we have expressed is stated without an interweaving. But what happens to be this sort would most seem to be things stated contraries by virtue of an interweaving. For 'Socrates is healthy' is contrary to 15 'Socrates is sick.' But not even in respect of these is it always necessary that one be true and the other false. For if Socrates exists one will be true and the other false, but if he does not, both will be false. For neither Socrates being sick nor Socrates being healthy is true on the whole with the non-existence of 20 Socrates. In respect of privation and habit, on the whole if the thing does not exist neither is true, but even if it exists it is not always true that one or the other is true. For 'Socrates has sight' is opposed to 'Socrates is blind' as privation and habit, and with Socrates existing it is not necessary that either one be true or false, for when he does not yet naturally possess it, both are 25

33

false, and on the whole if Socrates does not exist both again are false, both his having sight and his being blind.

But in respect of affirming and negating, always, whether
30 the thing is or is not, one is true while the other is false. For 'Socrates is sick' and 'Socrates is not sick,' it is apparent, both with Socrates existing, one is true and the other false, as well as with Socrates not existing, similarly. For if he does not exist, his being sick is false, but his not being sick is true. So that in re-
35 spect only of these [things opposed as affirming and negating], it must be proper that always one is true and the other false.

11. Of necessity the contrary to good is evil. This is evident
14a by induction of particulars, as to health the contrary is sickness, to justice injustice, to courage cowardice, and similarly with the others. But the contrary to evil is sometimes good and some- times evil. For lack which is evil has for its contrary excess which
5 is evil. And the mean being good, is in the same way contrary to each. Something of this sort is proper to few, but in respect of most the contrary to evil is always good. Moreover, in respect of contraries it is not necessary that if one exists, the remaining exists also, for with everyone healthy there will be health but no
10 sickness. Similarly with everything being white, there will be whiteness, but no blackness. Moreover, if 'Socrates is healthy' is the contrary of 'Socrates is sick,' and it is not possible simultane- ously for both to be attributed to the same person, it will not be possible with one of these contraries existing for the remaining to exist as well, for if 'Socrates is healthy,' it must not be that
15 'Socrates is sick.'

It is evident also, then, that contraries naturally arise either in the same form or the same genus. For sickness and health arise in the body of an animal, whiteness and blackness simply in a body, justice and injustice in a soul. And it is necessary that all
20 contraries either be in the same genus, or be in contrary genera, or be themselves genera. For the genus of white and black is color, but justice and injustice are in contrary genera, for the
25 former belongs to virtue and the latter to evil, and good and evil

34

are not in a genus, but happen themselves to be genera.

12. One thing is stated prior to another thing in four ways. First and most commandingly one is prior by virtue of time, by virtue of which one thing is stated older and more ancient than another, for older and more ancient are stated by existing in more time. 30

Second, what does not turn about by virtue of the sequence in being, as one is prior to two. For if two exists straightaway one sequentially exists, but from the existence of one it is not necessary that two exists, so that the sequence is not turned about and the existence of the remainder does not arise from the 35 existence of one, and that sort of thing seems prior upon which the sequence in being is not turned about.

Third, something is stated to be prior by virtue of some order, as in respect of sciences and arguments. For in the demonstrative sciences what are prior and posterior are attributed in order, for [in geometry] the elements are prior to the diagrams 14b in order, and in grammatical science the elements are prior to the syllables. The same way in respect of arguments, for the introduction is prior in order to the narration.[43] Moreover, besides what have been expressed, what is better and more honored 5 seems to be by nature prior. And the many are accustomed to saying that those who are honored and more cherished are prior to them. But this is nearly the most alien of the ways in which prior is stated of things.

The ways, therefore, in which prior is stated are so many. 10 And it would seem that besides what has been expressed there is another way. For of the things that turn about by virtue of sequence in being, what is in any way the cause, it is likely, might be stated by nature to be prior to the other. And it is evident that there are certain things of this sort. For being human turns about, by virtue of sequence of being, in relation to the true 15

43. Holding of fiction also, as the *Poetics* says the plot is an argument, λόγος, even if at times the words be mere speech, φάσις.

argument concerning this. For if human exists, the argument by which we state that human exists, is true, and these turn around. For if the argument is true by which we state that human exists,[44] then human exists. But the true argument that human
20 exists is in no way the cause of the being of the thing, though it is apparent that in a way the thing is the cause of the argument being true. For it is by the thing existing or not, that the argument states the true or the false. So that it is by virtue of five manners that we might state one thing is prior to another.

25   13. Things are stated simultaneous, simply and most commandingly, whose genesis is in the same time. For neither is prior or posterior to the other. These things are stated simultaneous by virtue of time. By nature those things are simultaneous which turn about by virtue of their sequence in being, one being in no way the cause of the being of the other, as in respect of
30 double and half. For these turn about, for half exists in reference to double and double exists in reference to half, but neither one is the cause of the being of the other.

Also the things that are divided against one another in the same genus are stated by nature simultaneous. By this is stated being divided against one another by virtue of the same dividing,
35 as what is winged, what is footed and what is in water. For these are divided against one another as being from the same genus. For animal is divided into these, into winged, footed and en-
15a watered, and none of these is prior or posterior, but things of this sort seem to be by nature simultaneous. Each of these again might be divided into forms, as footed, winged and enwatered. These then will also be by nature simultaneous, being from the
5 same genus and by virtue of the same dividing.

But genera are always prior to forms, for by virtue of the

44. Things either exist or not, arguments are simply true or false. Λόγος should not be translated 'speech.' For argument, not speech, φάσις, is 'that by which we know that something is.' Speech is the material of argument, as dough is the material of bread.

sequence of being it does not turn about, as animal exists prior to being enwatered, but what is enwatered does not necessarily exist prior to animal. Therefore, those things are stated simultaneous[45] by nature that, while they turn about by virtue of their sequence of being, are in no way the cause one of the other's being, as well as the things divided against one another from the same genus. But those things are simultaneous simply of which the genesis is in the same time.

14. Of motion there are six forms, genesis, destruction, increase, decrease, alteration, change of place. It is apparent except for one, these motions are other than each other, for genesis is not destruction, nor increase decrease, nor change of place, and so on with the others, but there is a certain problem with alteration, if it be necessary for what alters to be altering by virtue of some of the other motions. But this is not true. For nearly all, or most, passions happen to be altering in us, while associated with no other motions, for it is not necessary for what is moved by virtue of passion to be increased, nor decreased, and so with the others, so that alteration must be other and apart from the other motions. For if they were the same, what alters needs to straightaway also increase or decrease or follow any of the other motions. But this does not necessarily happen. So also what increases or is moved by some other motion, alters, but some things increase which do not alter, as a square is increased if a gnomon[46] is placed around it, but it does not become altered. So also with other things of this sort. The motions therefore are other than one another.

Simply, motion is the contrary of rest. But by virtue of particular motions, the contrary of genesis is destruction, the con-

10

15

20

25

30

15b

45. This shows clearly that ἅμα does not literally refer to time. Neither the Greek ἅμα nor the Latin simul was restricted to togetherness in time, for they meant sameness in any order of priority. English dictionaries have reduced the genus to one of its species.

46. A gnomon is that by which a parallelogram is increased or decreased by increasing or decreasing the length of its two sides.

37

trary of increase is decrease, to change of place rest in place
5 seems most to be opposed, and if change then to the contrary
place, as to down up, to up down. To the remaining of the
motions rendered, [i.e. alteration], it is not easy to render what
the contrary is, and it is likely there is no contrary, if it is not
10 rest by virtue of what sort, or change to the contrary of what
sort, as by virtue of change of place, rest by virtue of place, or
change to a contrary place. For alteration is change by virtue of
what sort, so that it is opposed by motion by virtue of what sort
15 or rest by virtue of what sort, or change to the contrary of what
sort, as white becomes black. For this alters by becoming a
change to the contrary of what sort.

15. Possessing is stated by virtue of many manners. For it is
stated as habit and disposition and certain other qualities, for we
20 are stated to 'have' science and virtue, or as 'having' how much,
such as one happening to have size. For one is stated to 'have' [a
size of] three pechus[47] or four pechus. Or as things concerning
the body, such as 'having' a cloak or tunic. Or as 'having' in a
part, such as having a ring on the hand. Or as 'having' a part,
such as hand or foot. Or as 'having' something in a vessel, such
25 as a medimnus[48] of wheat or a pipkin[49] of wine, for a pipkin is
stated to have wine and a medimnus wheat. Therefore, these are
stated to have as in a vessel. Or as something acquired. For we
are stated to have house and land. And we are stated also to
have wife, and wife to have man. And this now seems to be the
30 most alien (altered) way to express possessing, for by having we
signify nothing other than that one lives with a woman. Perhaps
some other ways of possessing might appear, but the things we
are accustomed to speak of are nearly all accounted for.

47. A pechus is a unit of measure modeled on the length of the
forearm, as a 'foot' is modeled on the foot. The Greek yard.
48. The common measure for grain, about 12 gallons.
49. A clay vessel for which lexicons give no standard size.

ARISTOTLE'S

CONCERNING INTERPRETATION

1. First one needs to assume what is a name and what is an 1
expression,[1] then what is negating, affirming, declaring and argument.

Things existing in voice, then, are symbols of affects[2] in the
soul, and things written are symbols of things existing in voice.
And just as all humans do not have the same letters [of the al- 5
phabet], so they do not have the same voices. But the primary
things of which these are the signs, the affects of the soul, are
the same to all, and the things that are similar[3] [to these affects
of the soul] are also the same to all. These things have been
expressed in our arguments concerning the soul, for that [argument] is another undertaking.

    1. Ὄνομα, cognate to γιγνώσκω, 'to know,' signifies the known of
which predicating is made, ῥῆμα signifies what is expressed, ἐρῶ, of that
thing in the predicating. They are not 'noun' and 'verb,' for nouns and
verbs are simply linguistic analogues to these. Nor does 'verb' include
all predicated of the underlying thing, nor 'noun' include all the qualifications of the underlying thing. It is only at times that Aristotle speaks
of words, insofar as he speaks of the relation between words, voice, and
affects of the soul.
    2. A πάθημα, or 'affect' in the soul, its modification due to the
senses, in spite of Liddell and Scott, is not the same as an 'affection,'
πάθος. For while a πάθος, is the soul's undergoing of suffering, of being
modified, a πάθημα, is that modification considered as an entity in itself,
just as a νόημα is an object of understanding resulting from understanding, νοῦς. Aristotle distinguishes them at 1108a31, even if scholars don't.
    3. The 'things similar' are the things of experience to which our
understandings are 'like' in form.

As in the soul, there are at times things understood[4] without
10 being true or false, and then at times things to which one or the
other of these is necessarily attributed, so also in voice. For both
what is false and what is true concern synthesis and dividing.
Names and expressions themselves, then, are like things understood without synthesis or dividing, as what is human or white,
15 whenever there is not something added to them, being so far
neither true or false. And there is a sign of this, for 'goat-stag'
signifies something, but is in no way true or false, if 'not being'
or 'being' is not added, either simply or in respect of time.
    2. Name then is voice significant by virtue of agreement,
20 without time, of which no part is significant when separated. For
in 'beautifulhorse' the 'horse' signifies nothing in itself as it does
in the argument 'the horse is beautiful.' Simple names are not as
woven names, for in the former the part is in no way significant,
25 while in the latter the part wishes to be significant, but signifies
nothing in separation, as 'horse' in 'skiff-horse.'
    It is by virtue of agreement because by nature nothing is a
name, but only when it becomes a symbol, since ungrammatical
sounds such as those of beasts make something evident,[5] but
30 none is a name. 'Not human' is not a name, and indeed there is
no name laid down that one needs to call this, for it is neither
argument nor negation. Let it then be indefinable name. 'Of
16b Philo' or to Philo' and such things are not names but fallings
[inflections of names][6]. The argument of this is the same as by
virtue of the others, but with 'is,' 'was,' or 'will be,' the name is
not true or false, which the name always is, as 'of Philo is,' or 'of
5 Philo is not.' For nothing is either true or false in this way.

    4. Nóημα, the object as grasped by the understanding, νοῦς.
    5. Animal sounds do not symbolize, yet signify, make evident.
They are signs, not symbols, as clouds are signs of rain, not symbols for
it. Aristotle uses 'sign' as the spore or trail of an animal, 'whoa' to a
horse, but symbols are a convention of consciousness.
    6. What in Greek is rendered by inflectional endings, we render in
English with prepositional phrases.

40

3. Expression is what in addition signifies time, no part separately signifying anything, and is always a sign of something stated by virtue of something else. I state in addition it signifies time, as 'health' is a name, while 'is healthy' is an expression, for it signifies in addition being attributed now. [An expression] is always a sign of things stated by virtue of something else, as things predicated by virtue of what is underlying. I state that 'is not healthy' and 'is not sick' are not expressions. For while in addition they signify time and are always attributed by virtue of something, there is no name laid down for difference. Let this be an indefinable expression, in that they are attributed similarly to both what does and what does not exist. Similarly also 'was healthy' or 'will be healthy' are not expressions but fallings of expressions. These differ from expressions in that while the expression signifies in addition what is present, the falling signifies what are round about. Expressions themselves, then, of themselves state names and signify something, for he who states stands thought and arrests the one hearing. But they do not in this way signify if something is or not. For they are the sign of neither the being nor not being of the thing, nor express bare being. For in itself it is nothing, but signifies a certain synthesis which is not understood without the things put together.

4. Argument is significant voice of which some parts when separated are significant as saying[7] but not as affirming. I state, as human signifies something, but not that it is or is not, but will be affirming or negating if something else is added. But a single syllable of human does not. For neither is the 'ouse' in 'mouse' significant, but is now only voice. In the coupling it signifies, but not by virtue of itself, as was expressed.[8] Every argument is significant, not as an instrument,[9] but, as expressed, by virtue of

10

15

20

25

30

17a

---

7. 'Argument,' λογός, may or not commit itself, but its parts do not. In merely 'saying,' φάσις, there is significance without declaring, ἀπόφανσις, either by 'affirming' κατάφασις or 'negating' ἀπόφασις.

8. 16a22.

9. I.e. not as something organized having a nature, like a tool.

41

agreement. But not every argument is declarative, but only that in which is attributed being true or false. And this is not attributed in all, as a prayer is an argument, but this is neither true or false. 5 Therefore, let us dismiss the others, for the investigation of these is more appropriate to rhetoric or poetics. The declarative argument belongs to our contemplation now.

5. The primary declarative argument is affirming and next is negating. The others are one by being bound together. It is nec- 10 essary that every declarative argument be from an expression or a falling [of an expression], for an argument of human,[10] if 'being' or 'will be' or 'was' or something of this sort is not added, is in no way a declarative argument. Why is [the argument] 'animal, footed, two footed,' a certain single thing and not many, for it is not by expressing them nearly upon one another that they are 15 one. But expressing this is another undertaking. A declarative argument is one that makes evident one thing or that is one by being bound together, while those are many which make many things evident and not one or are not bound together. Let name and expression then be only saying, since it is not possible to express in this way any of the things evident in voice so that they are declared, either when being questioned by someone or 20 when choosing it oneself. Of these, there is on one hand simple declaring, as something stated by virtue of something or negated of something, and on the other what is put together, as a certain argument already synthesized.

10. The Greek λόγος, argument, should not be translated 'speech,' for speech is mere saying, significance without attribution, and even 'a' speech refers to a collection of individually significant terms apart from any unifying form. Nor should it be translated definition, which is only a species of argument. To call λόγος speech is like saying a house is the same as the bricks, to call it definition is like using the word dog for animal. Even if the argument he refers to here is thought best exempli- fied by a definition, ὁρισμός, still what he literally says refers to any 'saying,' φάσις, that might be made of the object, any signifying or pred- icating, even if accidental and not admissible as science.

6. While simple declaring is significant voice concerning the attributing or not attributing of something, as times are divided, affirming is declaring something by virtue of something, and 25 negation is declaring something to exist away from something. Since it is possible both to declare what is attributed as not attributed, and what is not attributed as attributed, and what is attributed as attributed and what is not attributed as not attributed, and to declare in the same way concerning times that lie outside 30 what is now, it is possible to affirm or negate everything that is affirmed or negated. Thus it is evident that every affirming has an opposed negating and every negating has an opposed affirming. And let this be a contradiction, an affirming and negating that are opposed. I state opposed those that declare the same thing by virtue of the same thing, not homonymously, and as 35 many other things of this sort as we additionally determine relative to the annoyances of the sophists.

7. Since some things exist by virtue of a whole, some are particular [or exist by virtue of each], I state what exists by virtue of a whole is what is naturally predicated of many , while what is 40 not is particular, as while human belongs to things by virtue of a 17b whole, Kallias belongs to things by virtue of each [or particulars), it is necessary that anything declared, as attributed or not, belong at times to what is by virtue of a whole and sometimes particular. If it is declared by virtue of a whole that something is or is not attributed of what is by virtue of a whole, these declarings are contrary. I state declaring by virtue of a whole in respect of 5 what exists by virtue of a whole, is such as all humans are white, no humans are white. But when they are in respect of what is by virtue of a whole, but not by virtue of a whole, they are not contraries, yet what is made evident are contraries. I state declaring not by virtue of a whole in respect of what is by virtue of a whole, is such as human is white, human is not white. For 10 human exists by virtue of a whole, but in the declaring is not used by virtue of a whole. For 'all' signifies not that the thing is by virtue of a whole, but that the declaring is. But to predicate

43

by virtue of a whole in respect of what is predicated by virtue of a whole is not true, for no affirming is true, if what is predicated
15 by virtue of a whole is predicated by virtue of a whole, as all humans are all animals.

What is by virtue of a whole signified of the same thing that is not by virtue of a whole, I state is then an affirming opposed contradictorily to a negating, as all humans are white, not all
20 humans are white, or, no humans are white, some humans are white. But affirming by virtue of a whole is contrarily opposed to negating by virtue of a whole, as all humans are just, no humans are just. On this account these are not simultaneously true, but the declarings opposed to these are possible in respect of the
25 same thing, as not all humans are white, and some humans are white. Therefore, contradictions by virtue of a whole concerning what is by virtue of a whole, are necessarily one true, the other false, and particulars also, as Socrates is white, Socrates is not white. But those in respect of what is by virtue of a whole and
30 not by virtue of a whole, are not always one true, the other false, for it is possible to express simultaneously that human is white and that human is not white, and human is noble and human is not noble. For if he is disgraceful, he is not noble, and if he is coming to be something, he is not. It might seem suddenly ab-
35 surd because 'human is not white' appears simultaneously to signify also that 'no human is white.' But these neither signify the same thing, nor are they of necessity simultaneously true or false. It is apparent that one negating is of one affirming, for the negating needs the same negating which indeed the affirming is affirm-
40 ing, and negate the same thing, either some particular or what is
18a by virtue of a whole, either by virtue of a whole or not. I state, such as Socrates is white, Socrates is not white, and if something else is negated or the same thing negated of something else, it will not be opposed but will be another of another. And the negating of 'all humans are white' is 'not all humans are white,'
5 that of 'some humans are white' is 'no humans are white,' and that of 'human is white' is 'human is not white.'

44

Therefore, that one affirming is contradictorily opposed to one negating, and what these are, has been expressed, and that contrary declarings are other than contradictory declarings, and what these declarings are, and that not every contradiction is either true or false,[11] and why, and when these contradictions are either true or false.[12]

8. Affirming and negating is one when it signifies one thing by virtue of one thing, either being by virtue of a whole of what is by virtue of a whole, or not similarly, as (1) every human is white, not every human is white, (2) human is white, human is not white, (3) no human is white, some human is white, if white signifies one thing. But if one name is laid down for two things, out of which one thing is not possible, the affirming is not one, as if one assumes cloak for horse and human, 'the cloak is white' is not one affirming nor is its negating one. For there is no difference between expressing this and 'horse and human are white,' and no difference between expressing this and 'horse is white' and 'human is white.' Therefore, if these signify more than one thing and are more than one declaring, it is evident that the first either signifies more than one or signifies nothing. For a certain human is not a horse, so that this is not a case in which it is necessary that [the halves of] a contradiction be on one hand true and the other false.[13]

9. Therefore, of things that exist or have come to be, it is necessary that either the affirming or the negating be either true or false. And a declaring by virtue of a whole, about either what is by virtue of a whole or particulars, is always either true or false, as we have expressed.[14] But if something is stated, of what is by virtue of a whole, but not by virtue of a whole, this is not

11. Minio-Paluello omits the negative, not informing the reader.

12. I.e. when they are contradictories and not contraries. 17b16-26.

13. The Oxford translation, instead of following the codices with the negative conclusion, affirms a contrary which does not hold, thus illustrating Aristotle's point just made, 17b16-26.

14. 17b26-29.

necessary. This has also been expressed.[15]

But when it is of particulars and what is going to be, the case is not similar. For if every affirming or negating is either 35 true or false, then also everything is necessarily either attributed or not. For if one says that something is going to be while another says the same thing will not, it is evident that one or the other of these is true, if every affirming is either true or false. For it is not possible in matters of this sort to attribute both simultaneously. For if it is true to express that something is white 18b or is not white, it is necessary that it be either white or not white, and if it is either white or not white, it is true either to say or negate. And if white is not attributed to it, he is false [who stated it white], and if he is false [in stating it white], white is not attributed to it. Thus it is necessary that either the affirming or the negating be true.

5 Therefore, nothing either is, or comes to be, either by chance or by happening in any way, nor will be or will not be, but everything exists of necessity and not whatever way it will happen. For either he who says is being true or he who negates. For in the same way it will either come to be or not. For what happens in any way happens no more in one way than it happens, or will happen, in another. Moreover, if something is white 10 now, it was true to express before that it will be white, so that it is always true to have expressed of whatever comes to be that it will be, and if it is always true to have expressed either that it is or that it will be, it is not such to not be or not such that it will not be. But what is not such as not to come to be, is unable not to come to be. And what is not able not to come to be, is what necessarily comes to be. Therefore, everything that will be neces- 15 sarily comes to be. Nothing, therefore, happens in whatever way nor exists by chance, for if it exists from chance, it does not exist out of necessity.

But it is not possible to state that neither [the affirming or

15. 17b29-37.

the negating] is true, such as that it neither will be nor will not. For first if the affirming is false, the negating is not true, and if the negating is false it happens the affirming is not true. And 20 related to this, if it is true to express that it is white and black, both need to be attributed, and if attributed then the next day, and then the next. And if it neither will be nor will not be the next day, it will not be whatever happens, as a sea battle, for the sea battle needs neither to come to be nor to not come to be. 25

These absurdities and others of this sort happen if indeed, of every affirming and negating, either those stated as by virtue of a whole of what is by virtue of a whole or of particulars, it is necessary of opposed declarings that this be true and that be false, and nothing that comes to be happens in whatever way, 30 but everything comes to be of necessity. So that one need not deliberate nor undertake anything, since if we produce this, it will be, but if we don't, it will not. For nothing prevents one from saying this will be in countless years, and another saying not, so that of necessity whatever of these it was true to express will 35 sometime be. But it makes no difference whether someone expresses the contradictory or does not express it. For it is evident things done are not this way by someone affirming or negating them. For they will not be or not be because of the affirming or negating, nor if this was countless years before or whatever 19a length of time. Thus if in all time things were such that something was true, it would be necessary for this to come to be, and each thing that came to be would always be be this way, so that it would come to be of necessity. For whatever someone has truly expressed will be, is not such as not to come to be, and of 5 what has come to be it is always true to express that it will be.

But what if these are unable to be, for we see that the principle of what will be comes from both deliberating and action, and that on the whole what is able to be or not exists in things that are not always in activity, in which both being and not being 10 is possible, and thus both coming to be and not coming to be. And there are many things that make evident to us that things

47

are this way, such as that this cloak is able to be cut in half and not be cut in half, but be worn out before then. Similarly it is
15 also able not to be cut in half, for one would not attribute wearing itself out if it were not able not to be cut in half. So of other comings to be also, as are stated by virtue of such potentiality.

It is apparent, therefore, that not all things exist or come to be from necessity, but some things happen which ever way, and
20 neither affirming or negating is more true, and while one may for the most part[16] be more possible, it is not impossible for the other to come to be and the first not.

Therefore, it is necessary that what is exists whenever it is, and what is not does not exist whenever it is not. But certainly neither 'all that is' exists of necessity nor does 'all that is not' not
25 exist of necessity. For it is not the same that all that is exists of necessity when it exists, and all that is exists simply of necessity. And similarly of what does not exist. And the same argument holds in respect of a contradiction. It is necessary that everything either exist or not exist, or will exist or will not. But certainly it is not possible to go through these and express which is neces-
30 sary. I state such as, of necessity a sea battle will take place tomorrow or will not. But certainly not that the sea battle will arise of necessity tomorrow, or of necessity not arise. But certainly it is necessary that it either arise or not arise. Thus since arguments are similarly true as things, it is evident that the things that are such as to be which ever way by chance and have con-
35 traries that are also possible, necessarily have a contradiction that also exists in a similar way. Which indeed is what happens in respect of existing things that do not always exist and non-existing things that do not always not exist. For of these it is necessary that the parts of the contradiction be true and false, but

16. And with this Aristotle has laid down the logical basis of the practical, which through dialectical argument derives what exists 'for the most part,' ἐπὶ τὸ πολὺ, from accepted opinion, rather than the contemplative which derives through demonstrative argument what exists of necessity from the nature of a thing.

certainly not that this or this is, but whichever way by chance, and one may be more true than the other, but certainly not already true or false. Thus it is evident that it is not necessary of 19b every opposed affirming and negating that one be true and the other false. For what holds of things that exist, does not hold of things that do not exist, but being able both to be and not be, are as we have expressed.

10. Since an affirming signifies something by virtue of some- 5 thing, and the latter is either a name or a non-name, what is one affirming needs to be one thing by virtue of one thing. Both name and the non-name were expressed before. For I state 'not human' is not a name, but an indefinite name, for it signifies one thing in an indefinable way, just as 'not being healthy' is not an 10 expression. Every affirming is made either of a name and an expression, or of an indefinite name and expression. But without an expression there is neither affirming or negating. For is or will be or was or comes to be or others of this sort, from what we have laid down, are expressions, for in addition they signify time. So that the first affirming and negating are 'human is' and 15 'human is not.' Next 'not human is' and 'not human is not.' Again, 'every human is' and 'every human is not,' 'every not human is' and 'every not human is not.' And the same argument holds in respect of times outside the now.

Whenever 'is' is a third thing, additionally predicated, the antithesis is stated in two ways. I state that in 'human is just,' the 20 'is' is the third thing that I say putting the name and the expression together in the affirming. Thus because of this there will be four [declarings], of which two, relative to affirming and negating, are privations by virtue of their elements, while two are not. I state that 'is' will be put in addition either to 'just' or to 'not 25 just,' so also with the negating. Therefore there will be four [declarings]. We might understand what is stated from what is diagramed. 'Human is just,' the negation of this, 'human is-not just;' 'human is not-just,' the negation is 'human is-not not-just.'

Human is just   Human is-not just

Human is-not not-just   Human is not-just

For in these 'is' and 'is-not' is put in addition to 'just' and
30 'not-just.' These therefore, as stated in the *Analytics*, are ordered
in this way.[17] Similarly if the affirming of the name be by virtue
of a whole, as 'every human is just,' the negating 'not-every
human is just,' 'every human is not-just,' 'not-every human is
not-just.'

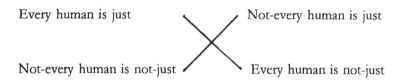

Every human is just   Not-every human is just

Not-every human is not-just   Every human is not-just

35   Except it is not possible in the same way for those across
the diagonal to be true together, though it is possible sometimes.
Therefore, these are two oppositions, but there are others if
something is added to what is underlying. Not-human is just,
not-human is-not just, not-human is not-just, not-human is-not
not-just.

Not-human is just   Not-human is-not just

Not-human is-not not-just   Not-human is not-just

20a   There are not more than these antitheses. These last are
separate by themselves, since they use not-human as a name.
     In respect of those in which the 'is' is not fitting, as in the
case of 'being healthy' and 'walking,' the same thing is done as

17. *Prior Analytics*, Book I, Chapter 46, 51b36-52a17.

we assumed when the 'is' was attached, as 'every human is 5
healthy,' 'every human is not-healthy,' 'every not-human is
healthy,' 'every not-human is not-healthy.'[18] For we must not
state 'not-every human,' but the 'not' in the negating must be
added to 'human.' For 'every' does not signify by virtue of a
whole but that the 'not-human' is by virtue of a whole. This is
evident from the following, 'human is healthy,' 'human is not- 10
healthy;' 'not-human is healthy,' 'not-human is not-healthy.' For
the name in the latter pair differs from that in the former in not
being by virtue of a whole. Thus the 'every' and the 'not' signify
in addition nothing other than the name being by virtue of a
whole in the affirming and negating. The other parts therefore
need to be applied the same. 15
   Since the contrary negating 'every animal is just' is what
signifies 'not one animal is just,' it is apparent these will never at
any time be simultaneously true or about the same thing. But at
times the opposites of these will be, such as 'not-every animal is
just' and 'some animal is just.' And 'not one human is just' is 20
consequent to[19] 'every human is not-just,' and the opposite [of
the latter], 'not every human is not-just,' is consequent to 'some
man is just,' for it is necessary there be some just humans.
   It is apparent also of particulars, if it is true to negate what
has been questioned, it is also true to affirm, as 'is Socrates 25
wise?' and the answer is no, then 'Socrates is not wise.' But of
what is by virtue of a whole, the similar thing is not truely stated,
but the negating is true, as 'are all humans wise?' and the answer
is no, then 'all humans are not-wise.' For the latter is false, but
'not every human is wise' true. One is opposite, one is contrary. 30
   Names and expressions that are opposed by virtue of what
are undefinable, as those concerning not-man and not-just, might

18. Cf. 19b19. In ancient Greek, in verbs like ὑγιαίνω, to be
healthy, the 'is' is an inflection, and not a separate word as in English.
   19. For Y to be consequent to, ἀκολουθέω, or follow, ἕπω, X is
denoted by 'X implies or entails Y' in modern statistical logic, though
there is a great difference in the sophistical handling of existence.

seem to be negatings without names and expressions, but are not. For it is necessary that a negating always be true or false, 35 and he who expresses 'not-human,' if nothing more is added, expresses what is not more, but rather less true or false, than he who expresses 'human.' 'Every not-human is just' and the opposite to this, 'every not-human is-not just,' do not signify the same as the former. But 'every not-human is not-just' signifies the 40 same as 'not-human is not one just.'

20b   Changing the places of names and expressions signifies the same thing, as 'human is white' and 'white is human.' For if this were not so, there would be more than one negating[20] to the same affirming, but it has been shown that there is only one. For 5 the negating of 'human is white' is 'human is not-white,' and the negating of 'white is human,' if this is not the same as 'human is white,' is either 'white is-not not-human' or 'white is-not human.' But the former is the negating of 'white is not-human,' and the latter is the negating of 'human is white,' so there will be two 10 negatings for one affirming. It is evident, then, that the same affirming and negating arise from changing the places of names and expressions.

11. It is not one affirming or negating, affirming or negating one thing by virtue of many or many by virtue of one, if one 15 thing is not put together from many. I state it is not one if one name be laid down but the things from this are not one. Thus human is equally animal, two footed, tame, and from these also one thing arises. But from white, human, walking, nothing one arises. Thus neither if something is affirmed by virtue of these, is 20 there one affirming, but while the voice is one the affirmings are many, nor if these are affirmed by virtue of one, it is still many.

If, then, a dialectical questioning is a request for an answer, either a premiss or one part or the other of a contradiction, the premiss being one part of a contradiction, the answer relating to 25 the latter example must not be one, for neither is the question

20. 17b38.

52

one, nor insofar as true. These were expressed in the *Topics*.[21] Simultaneously it is evident that questioning the 'what it is' is not dialectical, for from the questioning given one needs to pick whichever part of a contradiction one wishes to declare. The questioner needs to additionally determine, whether human is this 30 or not.

Since some things that are put together are predicated as one with all the predication being from what are predicated separately, and some are not, what is the difference? For it is true to express by virtue of human he is separately animal and separately two footed, and as one, and that he is human and white, and these as one, but though he is a shoemaker and good it cannot 35 be stated as one that he is good shoemaker. For, though each is so, when put together, many absurdities arise. For by virtue of human it is true he is both human and white, so also all together. Again, if he is white, then also what is all together [is white], so that he will be white, white, human, and this will go on to infini- 40 ty. And again, musical, white, walking, and many things woven 21a together. Moreover, if Socrates is Socrates and human, then he is also human Socrates, and if Socrates and two-footed, then also two-footed human.

It is evident, then, that many absurdities happen to be stated 5 if one assumes simply that interweavings arise. Let us now state how things must be assumed. Things predicated, and things of which they happen to be predicated, stated by virtue of an acci- dent, either to the same thing or one to another, are not possible of being one thing, as human is white and musical, but white and 10 musical are not one. For both are accidental to the same thing. Nor, if it is true to express the white is musical, is it alike that the musical and white is one, for the musical is white by virtue of an accident, so that what is white is not musical. On this account neither is a shoemaker simply good. But an animal is 15 two-footed, for it is not by virtue of an accident. Moreover, nei-

21. *On Topics*, Book VIII, Ch. 7.

53

ther are those that inhere in something else. On this account, neither is what is white many times one, nor is human stated human, animal, and two-footed. For two-footed and animal inhere in human. But it is true to express something by virtue of
20 something and simply, as a certain human is human, or a certain white human is white. Yet not always, but when an opposition inheres in what is additionally laid down to which a contradiction follows, it is not true but false, as expressing human of a dead human. But whenever it does not inhere, it is true. Yet when it
25 does inhere, it is always not true, while when it does not inhere, it is not always true. As Homer is a certain something, such as a poet, does he then exist or not? For the 'existing' is attributed to Homer by virtue of an accident, for because if belongs to poet, but not by virtue of itself, the 'existing' is predicated by virtue of Homer. Thus, in those predicatings[22] in which there exists no
30 contrary, if arguments are stated instead of names, and predicated by virtue of themselves and not by virtue of an accident, it is possible to express something and simply of these truly. But of what does not exist, because it is able to be opined, it is not true to express that it is; for the opinion of this is not that it is, but that it is not.

12. Having determined these, one must examine in what
35 way negatings and affirmings of what is able or unable to be exist in respect of one another, of what is possible or not possible, and concerning both what is unable to be and what is necessary, for these have certain problems. For if of things woven together, the contradictions which are themselves opposed to one another, are ordered by virtue of being and not being,[23] as the
21b negating of 'human is' is 'human is not,' but not 'not-human is,' and the negating of 'human is white' is 'human is-not white,' but

22. This use of κατηγορία, as the activity of the subject, shows its meaning is not that of its English cognate, category.
23. I.e., the connecting verb is negated, not what is predicated, as the examples show.

not 'human is not-white.' For if the affirming or negating were by virtue of all, it would be true to express that wood is not-white human.[24]

If this is so, in those to which 'is' is not added, what is stated instead of the 'is' does the same thing, as the negating of 'human walks' is not 'not-human walks,' but 'human does not walk.' For there is no difference in expressing 'human walks' and 'human is walking.'[25] Thus if it is this way in all cases, the negating of 'what is able to be' is 'what is able not to be,' but not 'what is not able to be.' But it seems the same thing is able both to be and not be, for everything that is able to be cut or walk is also able not to walk and not to be cut. The argument is that everything that is able to be in this way is not always active, so that the negating is also attributed to this. For what is able to walk [the walkative][26] is also able not to walk, and what is able to be seen also not to be seen. But sayings that are opposed are not able to be true by virtue of the same thing. This, therefore, is not a negating. For it happens from these things, either the same thing is said and negated simultaneously by virtue of the same thing, or it is not by virtue of adding 'is' and 'is not' that sayings[27] and negatings arise. If, then, the former is unable to be, the latter must be able to be picked. Therefore, the negating of 'what is able to be' is 'what is not able to be.'

The same argument concerns also 'what is possible,' for the negating of this is 'what is not possible.' And in a similar way in respect of the others, such as 'what is necessary' and 'what is unable to be.' For these arise, as with respect to the others, by the addition of being and not-being to the underlying things,

---

24. The absurdity follows from the truth of one of a pair of contradictories, plus the falsity of 'wood is white man.'

25. In Greek ἄνθρωπον βαδίζειν vs ἄνθρωπον βαδίζοντα εἶναι, the indicative changed to a participle and the verb 'to be,' as in English.

26. Another inflection no longer possible in English.

27. Thus 'saying,' φάσις, is used either of non declarative or declarative voice, just as in English.

'what is white' and 'what is human,' so in these matters being arises as what is underlying, and 'what is able to be' and 'what is
30 possible to be' determines the addition, as in respect of the former what is or is not what is true, in the same way with these as with being able and not being able.

The negating of 'what is able not to be' is 'what is not able
35 not to be.' On this account it would seem things 'able to be' and 'able not to be' are consequent to one another, for the same thing is able to be and able not to be, for things of this sort are not contradictions of one another. But what is able to be and
22a what is not able to be are never simultaneous, for they are opposed. Nor are what is able not to be and what is not able not to be ever simultaneous. Similarly the negating of 'what is necessary to be' is not 'what is necessary not to be,' but rather 'what is
5 not necessary to be. The negating of 'what is necessary not to be' is 'what is not necessary not to be,' and that of 'what is unable to be' is not 'what is unable not to be,' but 'what is not unable to be,' of 'what is unable not to be' is 'what is not unable not to be.' And, by virtue of the whole, as was expressed, being and not-being need to be assumed as what is underlying, while making these things, [what is able, or possible or necessary] into af-
10 firmings and negatings by attaching being and not-being.

And one must suppose the following are sayings that are opposed:

able	not able
possible	not possible
unable	not unable
necessary	not necessary
true	not true

13. Assuming things in this way consequences arise by vir-
15 tue of argument. For 'what is possible to be' is consequential to 'what is able to be,'[28] and the latter turns about with the former, as well as 'what is not unable to be' and 'what is not necessary to

be.' Both 'what is not necessary not to be' and 'what is not unable not to be' are consequent to 'what is able not to be' and
'what is possible not to be,' and 'what is necessary not to be' and 20
'what is unable to be' are consquent to 'what is not able to be'
and 'what is not possible to be.' Let us contemplate as we state
from what is written below.

able to be	not able to be
possible to be	not possible to be 25
not unable to be	unable to be
not necessary to be	necessary not to be
able not to be	not able not to be
possible not to be	not possible not to be
not unable not to be	unable not to be 30
not necessary not to be	necessary to be

'What is unable' and 'what is not unable' are then contradictorily consequent to 'what is possible' and 'what is able' and
'what is not possible' and 'what is not able,' but in a turnedabout
way. For the negation of 'what is unable' is consequent to 'what
is able,' the affirming consequent to the negating. For 'what is 35
unable to be' is consequent to 'what is not able to be.' The affirming is 'what is unable,' the negating is 'what is not unable.'
    One must see how what is necessary exists. It is apparent
that it is not in this way, but contraries follow, and contradictories are separate. For the negating of 'what is necessary not to 22b
be' is not 'what is not necessary to be.' For it is possible for both
of these to be true of the same thing. For 'what is necessary not
to be' is 'not necessary to be.' The cause of its not being consequent similarly to the others is that what is unable is rendered
contrarily to what is necessary, though being the same ability. For 5

28. That possibility follows what is able to be implies that possibility is the more general notion, as being animal follows being cat.

57

if it is unable to be, this is necessary, not to be, but to not be. But if it is unable not to be, this is necessary to be. Thus if the former [what is unable to be or not to be] are made similarly to what is able and not, the latter [what are necessary] are from contraries, since what is necessary and what is unable signify the same thing, but as we expressed, in a way that is turnedabout.

10   Or are contradictories of what is necessary unable to lie in this way? For what is necessary is able to be. For if not, the negating is consequent. For it is necessary either to say or negate, so that if it is not able to be, it is unable to be. Therefore, what is necessary to be is unable to be, which is absurd. But what is 15 not unable to be is consequent to what is able to be, and to this what is not necessary is consequent. Thus it happens that what is necessary is not necessary, which is absurd. But what is necessary to be is not consequent to what is able to be nor is what is necessary not to be. For it happens that both [being and not being] 20 are possible, and of these whichever may be true, the other will no longer be true, for simultaneously they are able to be and not be. But if it is necessary either to be or not to be, it is not able to be both. It remains, therefore, that what is not necessary not to be is consequent to what is able to be. For this is true also by virtue of what is necessary to be. For the same thing comes to be the contradiction to what follows what is not able to be. For 25 what is unable to be is consequent to this, and what is necessary not to be, of which the contradiction is what is not necessary not to be. Therefore, the contradictories themselves are consequent to these in the manner expressed and nothing unable to be happens when things are assumed this way.

    One might have a problem whether what is able to be fol- 30 lows what is necessary to be. For if it does not follow, the contradiction is consequent, what is not able to be. And if one were not to say the contradiction is the same, it is necessary to state what is able not to be, which are both false by virtue of what is necessary to be. But again, the same thing seems to be able to be cut and not to be cut, and to be and not to be, so that what is

necessary to be will be possible not to be. But this is false. It is 35
apparent then that not everything that is able, either to be or to
walk, is also able to be the opposites, but with respect to these
this is not true. First, in respect of things able, but not by virtue
of argument, as fire is able to heat and has this power without
argument. The potentialities then existing with argument are
themselves concerned with many things and with contraries, but 23a
those that are without argument are not all of them concerned
with contraries, but as expressed, fire is not able to heat and not,
nor are those others that are always active. Yet some potentialities by virtue of things without argument are able simultaneously
to be opposites. But this has been expressed in the interests of 5
this, that not all potentialities are concerned with opposites, not
even those stated by virtue of the same form. Some potentialities
are homonymous. For what is able is not stated simply, but in
one sense because it is true as existing in activity, as able to walk
because one walks, and on the whole being able because already
by virtue of activity it is stated to be able, in another because it 10
might be active, as able to walk because it might walk. And this
latter is potentiality in respect of those things only that are able
to move, but the former is potentiality also in respect of things
immovable. It is true to express of both (1) what is already walking and active and (2) what is able to walk,[29] that it is not unable
to be walking or to be. While then it is not true to express what 15
is able in this [latter] way (2) by virtue of what is necessary simply, in the other way (1) it is true. Thus, since what is by virtue
of a whole follows that which is partial, what is able to be follows what is of necessity, though not in all cases. What is necessary and not necessary is perhaps the principle of all things either
existing or not existing, and all other things need to be investigated as consequent to these. 20

It is apparent from what has been expressed that what exists
of necessity exists by virtue of activity, so that if eternal things

29. 'The walkative,' as above, p.54.

are prior, activity is also prior to potentiality. And while some things are activities without potentiality, such as first substances, some are activities with potentialities, which by nature are prior 25 [to the potentialities], though later in time, and some are never activities but only potentialities.

14. But is affirming contrary to negating or is affirming contrary to affirming, and argument contrary to argument, and is one stating that 'every man is just' contrary to 'no man is just,' or 30 is 'every human is just' contrary to 'every human is unjust'? As Kallias is just, Kallias is-not just, Kallias is unjust, which of these is contrary? For if the things existing in voice are consequent to those in thought, that opinion is contrary which concerns what is contrary, as that 'every human is just' is contrary to 'every human 35 is unjust,' and it is necessarily similar in the case of affirmings in voice. And if that opinion is contrary which concerns what is contrary, then an affirming will not be the contrary of an affirming, but the expressed negating. Thus we must examine[30] what sort of true opinion is contrary to a false opinion, whether it is opining the negating, or opining the contrary.

40 I state the following. There is a true opinion of the good, 23b that it is good, and another false opinion that it is not good, and another one that it is evil. Which of these is contrary to the true? And if they are one, by virtue of which does the contrary exist? To suppose that contrary opinions are defined by being concerned with contrary things, is false. For the opinion of the good that it is good, and the opinion of the evil that it is evil are per- 5 haps the same and true, either many or one, and these things are contrary. But contraries are not contrary by being concerned with contraries, but rather by existing in a contrary way.

If while there is the opinion of the good that it is good, there is the opinion that it is not good, and the opinion that it is

---

30. 'To examine,' σκοπέω, is always used of that 'fact,' τὸ ὅτι, that one 'seeks,' ζητέω, but 'to investigate,' ἐπισκοπέω, is always used of the 'why,' τὸ διότι, of which one 'inquires,' ἐπιζητέω.

something else not attributed nor such as to be attributed, we must assume [as the contrary] none of the latter, not those opined to be attributed that are not attributable, nor those not 10 opined to be attributed that are attributable, for both go to infinity, both those opined that are not attributable, and those not opined that are attributable, but [only] those in which deception exists. And these are the same as the things from which geneses arises,[31] and geneses arise from things opposite, so that deceptions also arise from opposites. If then the good is both good 15 and not evil, the first exists by virtue of itself, the second exists by virtue of an accident, for not being evil happens to the good.[32] But of each thing what is more true is that by virtue of itself, and if indeed this holds of the true, then of the false also. Therefore, the opinion that the good is not good is false concerning what is attributed by virtue of itself, while the opinion that it is evil, is false by virtue of an accident, so the falsity of 20 the negation of good must be more false than the falsity of the contrary. But he is most completely false concerning each matter who holds the contrary opinion, for contraries are among the things differing most concerning the same thing. Then, if of two opinions that are contrary [to a true one], the one that is concerned with the contradiction is more contrary, it is evident that this must be the contrary. The opinion that the good is evil is 25 woven together, for perhaps it is necessary also to be [first] convinced that the same thing is not good.

Moreover, if it needs to be similar in other cases, it would also seem to have been expressed well in this case, for the contrary concerns contradiction everywhere or nowhere. In those opinions to which there is no contrary, that opinion is false which is the opposite of the true, as he is false who supposes 30 man is not man. Therefore, if the contraries are these, the other contraries also concern the contradictions.

31. Both error and genesis exchange one opposite for another.
32. For things other than the good are not evil.

Moreover, the case is similar between the opinion that the good is good and the opinion that the not good is not good, and
35 in addition to these, the opinion that the good is not good and the opinion that the not good is good. Therefore, since it is true opinion that the not good is not good, what is the contrary? For stating that the not good is evil is not the contrary, for this would be simultaneously true, and the true are never contrary to the true. For it is possible for something not good to be evil, so that it is possible for these to be simultaneously true. Nor is the contrary that the not good is not evil, for this is also possible of being true, for the same thing might be these simultaneously. It
40
24a remains, then, that the contrary of the opinion that the not good is not good is the opinion that the not good is good, for this is not true. Thus also the opinion that the good is not good is the contrary of the opinion that the good is good.

It is apparent, then, that it will make no difference if we assume the affirmation to be by virtue of a whole. For the con-
5 trary is negation by virtue of a whole, as the contrary to opining that everything good is good is the opinion that nothing good is good. For the opinion that the good is good, if the good is by virtue of a whole, is the same as opining what is good is good. And this is no different than the opinion that everything that is
24b good is good. Similarly also in respect of what is not good.

Thus if it is this way in respect of opinions, and affirmations and negations in the voice are the symbols of those in the soul, it is evident that negation by virtue of a whole concerning the same thing is the contrary of the affirmation, as that every-
5 thing good is good, or that every man is good, or that nothing, or no one, and contradictorily, that not everything, or not everyone. It is also apparent that it is not possible for the true to be contrary to the true, neither opinions nor contradictions. For while contraries are concerned with opposites, it is possible for the same thing to be true concerning the same thing, and it is not possible simultaneously for contraries to be attributed to the same thing.

THE PHILOSOPHY OF ARISTOTLE

AND THE PLACE OF LOGIC IN IT

The writings Aristotle left to posterity, as in the case of Plato, are traditionally distinguished into those published during his lifetime, called exoteric, and those found among his possessions after he died, called esoteric. By one of those incredible twists of fate, and due in part to the Romans' burning of the library at Alexandria, all that we now have of Plato are those he published, while all we have of Aristotle are those not intended for publishing.

It was speculated long ago by unobservant scholars that Aristotle's writings are his lecture notes, and for centuries this guess was mechanically repeated by pedants. But the evidence is overwhelming that this is not true. For they are far too crabbed, difficult, cryptically precise, and personally couched, to be intelligible to students. Even his notion of teaching, both by reputation and by what his writings tell us of education, preclude much lecturing, but especially from notes as unsuitable for lecturing as these. He was called the 'peripatetic' because of his penchant for strolling through the gardens while teaching, and this accords far more with an easy dialectical exploration of a problem than the formal and pedantic stance effected by lectures.

None of his writings lend themselves either to being read to students, or to reminding the teacher of the phases of his topic. And seldom do any, especially these treatises on logic called the *Organon*, give an adequate notice of their purpose or procedure. For the arguments are extremely precise and demanding, yet the wording is abstruse and perplexing, full of ellipses and private code-like allusions, with little attempt to state or clarify its purpose or procedure. And they are far too detailed in their argumentation to function as notes needed to remind a speaker of his general order of topics or their salient points. These contradictory characteristics make them quite inhospitable to others but leave them quite accessible to the writer. Every translation goes to great lengths to make an opaque text readable to others. And it has been this very invitation to adumbrate that has been the scourge of faithfulness and accuracy of translation.

The combination of cryptic expression and detailed completeness of argument clearly indicates they had simply an archival function, the preservation of his arguments for his private reminder. How it was expressed was not as important as that it be expressed, for his understanding, not others. The only eyes meant to see them were his own, when he wanted to work things over, which he did constantly. For all of them show repeated reworking, referring back and forth to each other, without any of the priority that Jaeger had the temerity to claim. They were written as most creative thinkers write, from the necessity of putting thought into concrete form before it evaporates into forgetfulness, the way a painter needs to put brush to canvas, the way an architect needs stone and timber raised, especially a phenomenalist, for the sake of the completeness, ἐντελέχεια, of the thought. For a thought is hardly a thought until it is put in words. For until the words are chosen the thought is still potential. Only an academic pedant, out of touch with the learning process, could have thought these lecture notes. For notes outline, and do not go into details, unless one is so dull as to need everything spelled out. And anyone needing such minutiae is better off behind a counter filing papers, than trying to teach.

To talk of any topic implies some frame of reference, for both purpose and manner are infinitely variable. But if the frame used by a commentator is incompatible with is assumed by the writer he is commenting upon, there is no light shed on the writing, but only an advance of the commentator's agenda, and the logic of the writing is lost. For the history of thought shows that any ostensible topic displays different attributes under different purposes, presuppositions, and rubrics. It is the height of absurdity, if one means to explicate a man's thoughts, to employ a frame, convenient to the commentator, but unfamiliar or even contradictory to the writer's assumptions. The frame we use must be itself justified by what Aristotle himself says. We must find it justified by his statements, for there is little to choose between a known hostile approach to a philosophy and one that is simply misguided or irrelevant.

That such a frame exists is proved by the fact there is any dispute at all over the nature and purpose of logic. For there is no dispute unless those disputing have each found in what they say a common topic about which they make contradictory statements. Often as not, by simply going back in time, carefully examining the terms of the discussion, the common frame becomes visible. For example, logic gets its name from the verb λέγω, which is best understood, not by going to lexicons, but by examining the differences in the uses of related Greek words. For these days lexicons are written under the simplistic notion that its function is the search for substitutions, and therefore, because of the differences in languages, make as many as possible, without regard to their contradictory nature to one another in English, which has no parallel in the Greek word translated.

The Greek verbs referring to the act of speech differ, first, in whether or not they focus on the transitive. Some, like φημί, 'to say or speak,' tend to be used intransitively, not indicating so much that to which the speech refers, but simply reporting speech as uttered, φθέγγομαι, without implicating its assertive characteristic which focuses on the object, and simply viewing words as speech, φάσις. Even more obviously the verb ἐρῶ, 'to express or mention,' is used without an assertive relation to an object, and has an irregularity which reveals its primitive nature. For it has a present tense, εἴρω, but rarely uses it, and an aorist that is never used. Textbooks all blithely say that for these tenses the other verbs are substituted. But who is so omniscient as to say of the latter verbs, when they are used in their own right, and when they are used in place of the other? Such claims are made without thought. The primitive intransitive nature of ἐρῶ, is shown by the fact it derives from the verb 'to flow,' ῥέω, from which we get such words as 'rheumatism' which relates to catarrhal discharge, and rhythm, the flow of intervals. Even the words used in *Concerning Interpretation*, intending to relate words to reality, is that of 'expression,' ῥῆμα, to 'what has been named,' ὄνομα, related to γιγνώσκω, 'to know,' as a flow is related to what is stable by being known.

But for the act of asserting, or relating the speaker to topics or 'places' of discussion, things named, which is a transitive function, there are other verbs, that do not focus simply on the subject's activity, as intransitive verbs do, but focus on articulating the object it points to. (1) The verb of common parlance is λέγω, 'to state,' which does not at all mean simply 'to speak' or 'say' something, with emphasis only on the subjective. Even as the opening sentence says, it is an object or thing that is stated 'homonymous,' or any other predicate. And (2) κατηγορέω, 'to accuse or predicate,' explicitly emphasizes the transitive referential function, and (3) προσηγορέω, 'to address,' emphasizes making that assertion public. The first two, to state or predicate, are most used in designating attribution, or predicating an attribute of a thing. Λέγω has origins as complicated as ἐρῶ, coming from the notion of picking, or distinguishing, rather than flowing, which alone graphically illustrates the functional difference between the two sets of verbs relating to speech. From λέγω therefore come the articulating functions, like counting, reckoning, and the rational, λογικός, or what is productive of argument, as well as the faculty for doing this, λόγος, argument or reason. If one reads Plato and Aristotle carefully they are both highly sensitive to these nuances of the Greek, and chose between these words carefully. But scholars not worthy of the name are obtuse to their differences, and carelessly mix them up in translation. But astonishingly enough, no translator till now has seen this.

The logical function, then, is not simply the 'expression' of a content, but its 'articulation,' calling attention to what exists independently of speech. To state is to articulate and claim that something is 'out there,' part of an objective world. No translator has noticed that, if the Greek is read carefully, when there is no great emphasis on the objective referent of the speech, they use the words φημί, to say, or ἐρῶ, to express. But when they want it understood that a claim is being made about the objective nature of things, they regularly use the verbs λέγω and κατηγορέω. And if the Greek separates these functions, the English should also.

All philosophic or scientific procedures, concerned with the investigation of phenomena, either natural or the work of art and practice, are thus seen as ways in which a subject, the soul Aristotle might say, investigates or inquires into an object, the experienced phenomena, however those two may be interpreted. All procedures are some version of an assumed basic subject-object relationship. They differ as 'stating' anything of an object admits different procedures. We will explore how Aristotle does this differently than others. For above anything else, especially above the focus on conclusions, this gets us to a man's thoughts. Any difference in the conception of the relation between, or the nature of, the inquiring subject and the object inquired, produces all the disputes between alternative and competing philosophical and scientific procedures. That there might be other basic frames from which to discuss philosophic diversity, is not denied, but this one at least is basic, neutral, and inclusive, allowing the formulation of all possible positions without prejudice to the rest. We then ask, what considerations are used by Aristotle to formulate the relation between the inquiring subject and the object into which it inquires. For this question encompasses all that any logic attempts. For logic is the analysis, not of fact, but of the procedure by which anything claimed is shown factual. It is an analytical, not a factual, defense of argument. For that by which we investigate fact is not itself factual, though it must be concordant with fact, else the inquiry becomes a begging of the question.

Most of Aristotle's writings are his investigations of the phenomenal world, though he was also known as a poet. Scientific investigations of phenomena, he says, are attempts to formulate the 'why' or 'because of which,' διότι, of the 'fact' or 'the that,' ὅτι, which comes through perception and constitutes mere history. Every scientific statement therefore is part of either the formulation of fact, or the establishment of the 'why' or 'cause,' αἴτιον, of 'fact.' Aristotle affirms this in the *Posterior Analytics*, and in our first book on Aristotle, in 1961, we first showed that the statement is to be taken literally. But few commentators have understood that every scientific claim is about why fact exists as it does. On the nature and adequacy of one's conception of cause, therefore, does all difference in procedure depend. Every variability in the nature of cause permits a comparable variability in the nature of the procedure of science. This is the supreme condition of inquiry that Richard McKeon, who devoted so much of his life to procedure, or what he called 'modes of thought,' never grasped. In fact, in 1959, before my book was published, he denied it several times in discussions we had.

This immediately introduces a distinction between two sorts of statements about the world, those which are merely historical, expressing the facts of experience, and those which are scientific, possessing the causal evidence of fact. Those stated without the causal evidence of other statements, are either statements considered to need such evidence, or those considered self-evident which can then be used in science as the evidence for those needing it. This leads to a distinction between two sorts of intellectual faculties of which scholars have been totally unaware. In Greek, for every Greek writer, statements lacking the supporting evidence of other statements are said to be understood, νοέω, and their collection is called history. Those statements given methodological support of self-evident statements are said to be argued, συλλογίζομαι, διαλέγομαι, διαλογίζομαι, etc., and therefore subject to argument or reason, λόγος. This is the difference between the immediate or intuitive faculties, like understanding, νοῦς, comprehension, σύνεσισ, consideration, γνώμη, and judgment, κρίσις, and the mediate or discursive faculties, like reason or argument, λόγος, calculation, λογισμός, prudence, φρόνησις, etc. But till now no scholar has grasped the incredibly important difference between the immediate, intuitive faculties, such as described in Book I of the *Metaphysics*, and Ch. 19 of Book II of the *Posterior Analytics*, and the discursive, mediating faculties used in the building of the sciences, such as described throughout the rest of Book I of the *Posterior Analytics*. The immediate faculties are like perception and operate without our will and are therefore divine, since they are without error. For god understands and, in spite of British scholars, does not think or reason, while as the ethics says the function of the human is the discursive faculty, reason and thought, which can be in error.

The difference between a fact, ὅτι, that is understood, and a cause, αἴτιον, or 'why,' διότι, grasped by reason, in spite of the contradictory statement made by Liddell and Scott, is the difference between what is merely seen, εἴδω, by the understanding, and what is known, γιγνώσκω, by reason. For to know a fact is either to grasp a self-evident principle, or to have the cause of fact. Contrast this with Karl Popper's sophistical test concerning predictions, reducing the contemplative to the rhetorical, and one has one's first glimpse into derivative or reductive procedures to be distinguished below. What is 'seen' by the understanding is either practical particulars or contemplative matters that exist καθόλου, 'by virtue of the whole,' mistranslated as 'universal.'[1] For it is the understanding, νοῦς, or some related faculty, and not perception, that grasps from experience the 'first things' from which reason, λόγος, constructs science. The 'given' or facts from which science starts are not particular perceptions, as simplistic

1. Καθόλου does not mean 'universal,' for what is true of 'all' is not necessarily true of a 'whole,' of the thing as such. Cf. *Posterior Analytics*, 73a28 and 73b26. 'By virtue of a whole' adds 'by virtue of itself' to 'by virtue of all,' and the English word 'universal' does not convey this.

or reductive philosophies like those of Ayer or Carnap say, but 'wholes' understood, for it is wholes that explain parts, not the reverse. And the study of the procedure through which science goes has been called logic, because, as we said, reason or argument, λόγος, expressed as 'stating,' is the instrument, ὄργανον, by which what is given and 'seen,' εἴδω, by either perception or understanding, is turned to what is 'known,' γιγνώσκω, through or by virtue of one's grasp of why.

Such 'factual' sciences, the rational investigation of what is given, Aristotle divided into two kinds, depending upon whether the facts of the topics discussed exist through their own nature, are natural, or are artificial, formed by an external source like man. The first kind can only be contemplative in nature, and knowledge of what exists by nature alone exists for its own sake. The second, the practical sciences, are sought either for the sake of bringing things into existence, or for the sake of determining action apart from its product. For productive sciences seek knowledge only to alter what one finds into what one wants, while the practical sciences seek knowledge as a guide to action.

He made these distinctions, not as some superficial wits have said, because he had a penchant for classifying, but because the procedures by which these differing problems are both understood and solved are so different as to necessitate their distinction, for you can't brew coffee by baking bread. The use of a procedure germane to one area aborts one's purpose in another. The primary distinction between the contemplative and practical sciences is only accidentally a distinction in things, and primarily a difference in procedures responding to circumstances.

To treat Aristotle's procedure as a specific formulation of the relation between inquiring subject and inquired object is convenient, both to his own basic distinctions, and to the common origin of all philosophic thought, and is also an important consideration in grasping his own place historically. For it also properly articulates his opposition to Plato, who dominated his intellectual life from the age of 17, in 367 B.C., to the age of 37, in

347 B.C., when Plato died at the ripe old age of 80.

There is hardly a work of Aristotle that does not, at least by implication, work in conscious declination from the overpowering influence of Plato. Perhaps, only if one is as consumate a thinker as Aristotle, might one grasp the import of such an influence, both positively as an exhortation to Aristotle's native tendencies, and negatively as an abrasive to those tendencies. Perhaps the power of his response to Plato, given the natural opposition of their directions, is only what one would expect as fitting response to Plato's genius, like the successful bat turning the advantage of the pitcher against himself.

For the distinction between the subject and the object, though necessarily granted at the beginning stages of inquiry, is ultimately a spurious distinction for Plato, to be overcome finally when reality is grasped in a way that approaches adequacy. For in Plato there is no ultimate distinction between object and subject, between the world that is known and the knower of that world, for what exists is intelligence. But in Aristotle the most profound error that can be made in science, even practical science, is the confusion of what we inadvertently contribute to the inquiry and what is objectively out there. The separation of the knower from the known is the first condition of knowledge for Aristotle, the ultimate height of misdirection for Plato. Democritus and Protagoras give the logically remaining two alternatives, the former reducing the knower to an epiphenomenon of the known, the latter reducing the known to a perspective of the knower.

This ultimate impossibility of distinguishing the inquiry into inquiry from the inquiry into the thing inquired, makes impossible a separable logic for Plato. As the 7th Epistle says, outside an argument there is little to say. In the dialogues of Plato the soul continuously reflects on its own operations, for only a mind conscious of its own operations succeeds at anything. But it is only under the aegis of a method like Aristotle's, which separates the procedures of the inquirer from the nature of the thing into which he inquires, that the possibility arises of a separate logic.

Thus whether or not logic is separable from science depends upon whether the methods of inquiry are supposed many or one, and therefore for both single method procedures, the dialectical and the operational,[2] logic is not separable from science. For whatever is appropriate for the object is appropriate for the subject, but for drastically different reasons in the two. For Plato's dialectic makes the subjective and the objective one, but the sophists made all subjective by denying the reality of the objective. The other method, the logistic followed by Democritus, being also multi-method, also separates logic from science, but Aristotle made the subjective and objective of equal procedural importance, while Democritus reduced the subjective to an illusion, as the logical positivists said all we need are facts.

For Aristotle, then, logic, unlike physics or ethics, is not a seeking for, ζήτησις, or examining of, σκέψις, fact, or what is given, τὸ ὅτι, much less an inquiring for, ἐπιζήτησις, or investigating of, ἐπίσκεψις,[3] cause, but an analysis, ἀνάλυσις, of the considerations necessary to achieve what inquiry seeks. These considerations are the conditions under which anything is justifiably 'stated.' They depend neither on the nature of language, or on the reality of the things of this world. One may look to the customs of man's 'stating' things, but 'logical truth' is merely the consistency of stating for an assumed function, what Kant has taught us to call 'analytical truth.' Reflection on stating, logic or procedure, makes each performance of stating better. But one does not learn the analytic skills of logic at the same time as employing them in some science, as he says, *Metaphysics*, 1005b2-5, which is what Plato and the sophists would have us

2. We borrow some terms from Richard McKeon. Though he never stated so, the ones for which he had a defendable and valid use can, in function, all be derived from Aristotle.

3. Scholars have never noticed the precision of the Greek. The first two relate solely to fact, those with ἐπί, 'in respect of,' as indicated, relate to the predicated cause. The verb chosen thus gives indication of the phase of procedure being pursued, history or science.

do, for they are presupposed in doing the science. Yet Aristotle and Democritus presuppose logic by differing procedures.

The *Organon* is, therefore, the scientist's consciousness of his own operations, the reflexivity of the inquirer, thinking about his own thinking, or arguing about arguing. But this is quite different than the divine, which reflexively, through immediate understanding, not discursive reason, understands its own understanding. We call it logic, after reason or argument, the discursive faculty, not noetic, after understanding, the immediate or intuitive faculty. The two differ since understanding, νοῦς, as he says at 1072b22, 1174b15, 25, and 33, is the function of the divine which is pure activity without the encumbrances of the space-time continuum, form without matter. But at 1177b26 he says this is too strong, κρείττων, 'by virtue of' the nature of the human, who must understand in this world only by abstraction from perception, and whose function as a soul in a body is determined at 1098a13 to be the activity of reason. For while science may be based on understanding, it consists in the activity of reason. And human understanding differs from that of the divine which is a matter of immediate introspection, god's consciousness of his own existence being the basis of what he understands, while man's understanding, as both the *Metaphysics* and the *Posterior Analytics* say, is an abstractive process from perception, all that is available to a creature in space and time, and far inferior. This means, that though reasoning in science is based on principles grasped by the understanding, understanding, in the case of man, comes slowly, painfully, and imperfectly, through a dialectic, as outlined in the *Topics*. In this, reason, in a second best procedure, and not demonstratively as in the two *Analytics*, separates the false from the true to grasp the beginnings or principles on which science is based.

But when today it is said the *Organon* constitutes Aristotle's logic, there are serious problems that immediately come to the fore. The *Organon* is certainly not the logic that most students see when they take courses of that name, though here and there one might find similarities. For Aristotle would hardly think that most text books on logic have much to do with any rational approach to the solution of the problems of science. This is partly because modern texts on logic, in attempting to accommodate themselves to all notions of procedure in the sciences, adequately conform to none. They are also abundantly affected by two tendencies in thought against which Aristotle fought long and hard, the analytical atomists, Leucippus and Democritus, and the intellectual relativists, the sophists, between whose opposed positions those having the greatest effect on logic, like Bertrand Russell, and modern writers of logical text-books, continuously vacillate. The first is typified in method by Isaac Newton, John Locke, Gottfried Leibniz, Ivan Pavlov, John Broadus Watson, Max Plancke, and B. F. Skinner, the second by Galileo Galilei, Immanuel Kant, John Stuart Mill, Charles Darwin, Sigmund Freud, Niels Bohr, and Percy Bridgman. For these approaches have dominated western thought since Roman days. Treatises on logic are also not, as teachers of science seem to think, the procedures that scientists follow when making either their discoveries of fact, or alighting upon their explanations of fact, or what Popper in his reductive fashion equates with predictions. For logic is heuristic, not by its nature, but only in its sophistic versions. For there is no rational discussion of the adventitious manner in which the mind grasps its ideas.

But if one means the procedures that a scientist or thinker goes through in order to establish truth, proof, persuasion, insight or any other value, including Popper's reductive notion of prediction,[4] concerning a topic of inquiry, then the *Organon* is indeed Aristotle's logic. The word ὄργανον in Greek means 'instrument,' meaning that for bringing inquiry to warranted

4. 'Reductive' is not a disparaging subjective sobriquet, but the objective fact of procedurally limiting the possible objects of rational inquiry, which is not only an objective characteristic of the operational and logistic methods, but often advertised by them as their virtue.

claims. It is the first treatise in the history of civilization, whether north, south, east or west, that sets down, in a work separate from inquiries into fact, the stipulations of inquiry simply as inquiry. For, as we have already indicated in its opposition with Plato, it is only under rather special notions of procedure that the separation can be made. It is therefore due not only to his genius, but to his procedure, that Aristotle was the 'inventor,' if you will, of not only ethics, as we saw in our commentary on the *Nicomachean Ethics*, but of rhetoric, the several sciences, and logic. For though in his day other procedures than Aristotle's implied the separation of logic, as that of Leucippus, Democritus, and Empedocles, they did not, as he did, do the work.

Any hesitancy to call his *Organon* logic, and the main reason there were no other logics written before Aristotle, both lie in the extremely diverse nature of the procedures that have been touted as scientific. This diversity exists, not simply between different times and societies, but just as often within the same society, and not only in respect of science, but any rational procedure generally. To this diversity of procedure Chapter 10 of my commentary on Aristotle's *Nicomachean Ethics* and Chapter 1 of my commentary on Aristotle's *Metaphysics*, were addressed. What logic is for any particular thinker, is the amalgam of the immediate implications of that thinker's procedure in doing science or philosophy.

This is in fact what makes most courses on logic of questionable relevance, for, because of the incompossible ways of doing science, even today, there is no way to write about how inquiries are made rational, nor determine the nature of intelligence, without offending most of those doing it. Thus, in the effort to please the greatest number, logic texts are reduced to ineffectual simplicities or vacuous nonsense about a few confined areas about which there can be some agreement, usually only verbal. Text books in logic today have little in common either with Aristotle's notion of logic, or with the procedures by which most scientists establish their conclusions. Obviously they are therefore of little credit either to themselves, or to science. The only way a logic can be made relevant, is to ignore the diversity of scientific procedures, to assume one consistent mode and rigorously apply it. And this is precisely what Aristotle did.

But the other problem mentioned, not the diversities of logic, but the eclectic and unsupportable notions of logic, must also be addressed. Aristotle's logic often distinguishes between different ways of proceeding depending on the circumstances of one's inquiry, and it is sometimes assumed that method is the way discoveries are made, the theories at least, if not the facts themselves. But there is no way of reducing to a determinate procedure the considerations by which one lights upon ideas that explain the observed world. These are as fortuitous and haphazard as falling in love, and in fact a logician is no more able to guide a scientist in his search for explications, than a psychologist is able to guide one in the selection of a durable marriage. The explication is wrought from the tendencies of a thinker in implicating 'why,' or cause.

The notion of a science of the procedures of discovery is analogous to and as preposterous as the notion of a computer that thinks. For the enthusiasts of cybernetics that come to the conclusion that computers can think, do so only through their reductive understanding of the nature of thinking. This reduction is that effected generally by the logistic and operational methods, for only those using such procedures either make this claim for computers, or simplistically suppose that thinking can be quantitatively measured, as for example in intelligence tests. But computers cannot think in the complete sense of thinking, because they do things only according to procedures that are already programmed into them. Everything they do is thus hypothetical, based upon assumptions, not complete thinking, which must include the search for principles. To some considerable degree one might and in fact does program into a computer the conditions under which, the areas in which, and the rules by which, in certain confined problematic areas, solutions might be found. But this, as Plato showed us, is thinking 'hypothetically,' within the confinement of a frame of assumptions. Yet as Dewey expressed it, in the ultimate sense, and the sense that defines the condition without which there is not fully any thought or stating, but only some partial function of thought, thinking is the search for rules when all known rules fail, not some while leaving others to govern. By definition computers do not do this, for every function of a computer has the parameters of its operations fixed by its software or its CPU.

That is why 'establishing' truth or some other value is the function of logic, not the 'discovering' of it. For if the scientist's problem is first the search for 'fact' within his selected area, what Aristotle called its propaedeutic, or history, and second the organization of thought, the investigation, by which that body of fact can be said to be 'known,' the logical problem is completely restricted to the problem of the organization, the formation of that matter stated generally, without consideration of any particular body of fact. But this is precisely the separation that was impossible for Plato, for he was convinced that the rationality that knows is the rationality that is known. Therefore, to understand the possibility of such separation of the procedures of science from the actual inquiry of science, demands we continue with an explication of Aristotle's way of doing science.

The atomists like Leucippos and Democritus, in holding that knowledge necessitated a sharp separation between the factors necessary to explain fact and the facts to be explained, were in this respect like Aristotle, all differing from the sophists and the Platonists. But atomists thought that this explanation could be effected by a discovery of the simplest elements out of which all existences are compounded. Their very simplicity would be guarantee there had been no intrusion of the observer, and as long as the procedural steps were also simple, the compounds would be as objective as the starting points. By this procedure the interference and falsifying influence of the observer could be negated. Such procedure is found in many scientists throughout history including today's, the foremost example in history being, as we said, Isaac Newton. For the atomists, in this process all factors of the inquiring mind become not only 'epiphenomenal,' but all things consequent to any obtrusion by the mind prove to be unsuitable to scientific method. As a result all the practical activities of man fall within the domain of the irrational, since in those matters the reductive procedures of the sciences do not apply.

For Aristotle, however, to know is not to compose compounds from simples. It is not even necessary that simples exist. What is basic instead is the resolution of the functions of all the factors proper to a situation on the basis of the completion which all those factors attain and on which their separate function depends. This means all inquiry necessarily starts from the 'whole,' the 'completion,' τέλος,[5] of the topic. For it is the whole that explicates or makes necessary the part, not vice versa, as in reductive procedures. This is the significance of the τὸ τὶ ἦν εἶναι, 'the being that was,' or 'essence.' For if cause is a consideration by which reason explains fact, among causes there is a difference between those that are complete, τέλειος, and those that are incomplete and need the supplementation of other causes. Thus again we see that all variation in procedure relates to the range that the derivative[6] nature of cause makes possible.

In the *Metaphysics* Aristotle shows the material and formal causes explain what is static in phenomena, while 'that from which the motion,' or initiation, and 'that for the sake of which,' or completion, explain the dynamic in phenomena, i.e. its process or action. These characteristics of the causes are determinative, as we will see, of the procedures followed in each of the four pos-

5. In every commentary we have shown the harm in the failure of scholars, including Liddell and Scott, to understand the difference between τελευτή, end or finality, and τέλος, completion.
6. Things are derivative when there is a primary sense of the thing, as it is the body that primarily is healthy, and then other things are that thing, only in analogous or derived senses, as food, exercise, and the doctor are healthy by contributing to the body's being healthy.

sibilities, in each function of inquiry. This alone is proof that the procedure in each function is a consequence of the cause chosen, and that therefore McKeon had many of the facts concerning procedure correct, but not the reason for them. But neither the material nor the initiation of motion is adequate to the grasp of any 'whole' of which one speaks, whether static or dynamic. This is because, everywhere, wholes have properties not traceable to the parts or potentialities from which they arise, and initiations can be interrupted anytime by extraneous matters. Only when procedure is based primarily on either form or completion, does it have the capacity for the complete, though the formal cause by itself is the completion only of the static, which is incompetent of including the dynamic. Therefore it is only in the completion of any process, function, or action, that there is any possibility of incorporating everything it is possible to experience. By their nature, the procedure of the physiologists and atomists, making material primary, and that of the sophists, making initiation primary, are reductive procedures needing completion through the other two causes. The formal cause, which Plato hypostatized, is reductive by excluding motion.

The nature of that with which one starts, however, depends upon the nature of the problem. For the investigation of the reasons for a bolt of lightning crossing the sky, is a different kind of problem than determining how to make an implement to turn the earth over, and this is a different kind of problem than determining what to do when your son revolts against the rules you and your wife suppose he should live by. They are different, not because they are different 'things' in some big classification of life made by some encyclopedist, but because what each seeks to accomplish, and the factors needed to be taken into account in order to solve each sort of problem, are very, very different, with ver different logical relations, especially concerning the principles that control the different inquiries.

But however different these circumstances may be, some are similar, and even where factors are quite different, they still perform analogous functions in those different inquiries. For example, the function achieved might be different as well as the means to it, but there still will be the question of common means.[7] The problem, then, is to determine the common functions of all inquiry allowing for all variability.

In the optimum, when for some reality that has been isolated there is also a matching thought in the observer, there is also a word one uses that stands for that reality. It is the equivalence between thing, thought and word, at this optimum condition, that has allowed a periodic shift in the locus of philosophic problems. For throughout the recorded history of human thought, when philosophic problems have seemed unsurmountable and differences between schools of thought have seemed firmly entrenched, a few enterprising thinkers have called for a change in the general orientation of philosophic discussion, and the determination of which function of logic, and the assumptions it intails, is primary, whether principle, method, or interpretation. This was one of the factors in Richard McKeon's schema which were discussed in Chapter 10 of my commentary on Aristotle's *Nicomachean Ethics*, and in Chapter 1 of my commentary on his *Metaphysics*. Procedure was generally understood by the time of Kant, else he would not have been able to advocate his 'Coperican revolution,' but it was also well understood by Aristotle, as all his works show. But for many, including even some thinkers who have created notice, the matter is badly understood.

When the problems of the nature of existing things become apparently insoluble, a great innovator like Hume or Kant comes along and says we have been asking the wrong question. Since nothing can exist as known that is not known to a mind that knows, perhaps, they say, instead of seeking the nature of what

7. When thought is reductive, it seems that means are needed to achieve ends, but a little thought should make it evident we never wish an ending to either our efforts or the promise of things, but their completion or fulfillment. We are the victims of the rhetoric of our age.

is, we should seek the nature of the faculty that knows what is. As a result, metaphysics, which is the investigation of the things that are, has its life supports removed, and epistemology takes its place as the science of all science. When predictably this too fails, because there is no more agreement now than before, innovative thinkers like John Dewey and George Edward Moore tell us again we are on the wrong track and advise us to consider instead the linguistic or behavioral devices by which both these things and these ideas are expressed, and now semantics or pragmatics takes over, for all the structures we sought, first in the thing, then in the thought, can now presumably be more easily found in the knowledge of their statement or expression.

We have taken this little detour through thing, thought, and word, more elaborately developed in the two commentaries mentioned, because logic today is myopically thought to be about terms, propositions, and verbal structures called arguments. That is, philosophic problems are thought to be best approached by the consideration of semantic, semiotic, or pragmatic problems, the marks of knowledge rather than the things known or the faculties that do the knowing. They are thought to be matters of words, the symbols standing for both the things of this world and the thoughts in minds that grasp those things. Even in ancient Greek, the same word stands for (1) a rational structure that is found to exist, a ratio or proportion in things, (2) an intellectual faculty that grasps that rational structure, as well as (3) the verbal formulation in which that structure appears as a predication, for all of these are called λόγος, (1) ratio or proportion, if you prefer things, (2) reason, if you have an affinity for faculties, and (3) argument, if you are semantically inclined, though argument itself can be thing, thought or word.

But Aristotle was quite conscious, where his translators are not, that logic is no more about words than biology is merely about the words 'monkey,' or 'nervous system,' or 'membrane.' Most of the time, therefore, especially since Aristotle's orientation was to 'being,' rather than 'being known' or 'being stated,' for his

81

philosophy was metaphysical, not epistemological or semantic, even in his logic, he is primarily talking about realities, and not as we do, about the terms in which one talks about realities. Yet he does occasionally talk about terms, just as a biologist once in a while has to stop and say something significant about his terminology. The logician has to do this more often than the scientist, because of the general problem of all inquiry, that of finding thoughts and words apposite to the flux of changing phenomena. For, in spite of all the hullabaloo about experimental procedures, inquiry literally juggles words and ideas more than things.

Logic, then, for Aristotle, is primarily about the relationships between things just as science is, but not as occasioned by the nature of things. For if science discovers relationships between things in order to argue about what does and does not exist, it must do so within the parameters that logic provides, independently of fact, for the consistency of statements as such. For logic is as autonomous in its domain as is science, for the nature of things is not determined by the nature of speech or speaking, and the requirements of speaking does not depend on the nature of that of which one speaks, but on what we are trying to do.

And we might also add, that what is true of any logic by any procedure, is true as well of the general statements such as McKeon's about the schema of logical procedures. McKeon's schema can by its very nature be dependent upon no factual philosophical investigation, whether metaphysical, epistemological, or semantic, which is why Walter Watson's emendations of McKeon are so much in error, fn. 8, p. 85, below. For long after he wrote his book *The Architectonics of Meaning*, Watson wrote in another article, that he got his new archic variables from Aristotle's *Metaphysics*, clearly an erroneous source for any logical variable. For each logic must have the facility for expressing the gamut of human thought, and cannot be structured on what it thereby finds reality to be, since this would beg the question. Thus one may examine Aristotle's entire *Organon* without finding a single reference to any necessary metaphysical, epistemological or semantic existent. All of Aristotle's logical language is derived solely from the everyday, but precise, necessities of 'stating,' which is why it is called logic.

But translations of Aristotle's logic would never lead a reader to suppose this, for Aristotle's discussions about reality have been turned into discussions about semantic elements. The fact that man uses 'words' to manipulate 'things' in his 'thought' has been used by translators absorbed with a semantic approach to philosophy generally, to justify the assumption that Aristotle is as semantically oriented as we are. But if we are to understand precisely what Aristotle says, we shall have to be very careful in determining just what Aristotle is talking about.

With this proviso, then, Aristotle's *Organon* is a formulation of the procedures found in his scientific works. Science is not words in a book, but a power of the soul, 1b2, 8b29. Thus in many ways the *Organon* explains many of the things accomplished without explanation in the sciences. It covers the gamut of inquiry, whatever the nature of the topic. It provides for widely different purposes in inquiry, and equally wide treatment of the resources upon which argumentation is built. What all rational operations attempt, Aristotle said, is to discover the why of the fact. In this procedure different functions of reason can be distinguished which are equally pertinent to any rational purpose.

The Four Logical Functions

Aristotle found four logical problems in making any statement justified or defendable, so the logical problems addressed by any complete inquiry are also four. But Aristotle put his logical work in six treatises because one of those problems, being of greater concern with more sweeping consequences, had to be put into three, resulting in six works rather than four. The four are (1) the categorizing of things about which one talks into kinds of existence, (2) the interpretation of predications between things so as to make it possible for them to express fact, (3) the determination of priorities between statements so that some can justify or establish others, and (4) what that is on the basis of which they are established. The solution to these logical problems, as said, does not depend on the structure of the universe, but only on how one assumes statements are justified. Logic is thus about the procedural assumptions of the inquirer, not about the world. For the manner of determining the nature of the universe cannot be presumed to depend on what its nature is, for this would beg the question. It depends rather upon the predilections of the inquirer in accounting for what is, his notion of cause. The manner used in establishing these procedural necessities, the analysis of wholes into parts, is that which one version of procedure, that of structure, assumes to be the highest, or what governs all thought. But in Aristotle, as an example of his procedure's ability to encompass all the others, it is a procedure of restricted function, with limited accomplishments.

(1) *The Categories.* Since all inquiry into experience is an attempt to state, in a defendable way, why the things experienced are as they are, all inquiry must first determine what sorts are the 'things' of which statements are made. The history of thought, even as early as Aristotle's day, exhausted the variety of manners in which the 'things' talked about, can be regarded as things. When Aristotle gets to the treatises that treat the logical relations of these things or 'items' of discourse, the *Analytics*, he calls them 'limits,' ὅροι, which semantically inclined scholars erroneously translate as 'terms.' But as Liddell and Scott show, for any Greek other than Aristotle, an ὅρος is always an existing 'thing,' and never any linguistic element. It is only our penchant for thinking that philosophic problems are semantic that has led to this error, and only in Aristotle's case, because only Aristotle ever wrote works on logic. The categories or predicatings, are the 'accusings' we make of experience as consisting of 'things,' and the fact that these things are expressed in words is immaterial. If biology is not the study of the 'words' frog, membrane, and neuron, but the things signified by those words, then logic as the

84

study of the procedure by which such investigation is conducted, must also be the study of procedures concerned with things, and only secondarily about the words used to express them.

Each of the four problems of logic exists only because there is a latitude left to the discretion of the inquirer, as to how that problem may be dealt with. And the latitude in each case lies in what sort of thing is admissible as evidence in solving the problem. But evidence is always what someone regards as the cause of something being as one claims. Therefore all differences in procedure are differences in what is regarded as the cause of the thing one is explaining. The problem of the *Categories* is that of determining what are the 'things,' the items of experience, or 'limits' of inquiry. Whatever cause one focuses on in doing this, determines for that person what his categories are. The Anatolians and the atomists supposed 'things' were determined by the elements of which they are composed, and thus saw things as various 'matters.' The sophists supposed that 'things' are the projection of the speaker's point of view, and thus saw things as 'types' reflecting their origins or 'that whence the motion.' The Platonists saw 'things' as the forms imitated imperfectly in space and time, and thus saw things as transcending 'hierarchies' culminating in the most encompassing ideas. Aristotle's more encompassing suggestion is that the 'things' are a range of 'kinds' from the completely and independently existing to their incomplete accidents, and his *Categories* is therefore a listing of the different ways things exist, from substances, which exist independently, through the various dependent existents, which includes all those offered by the others. For a notion of what exists in completeness is able to articulate also what exists as matter, point of view, or form, since what exists in itself or completely includes also all the others. Starting with what exists completely, all other things can be accounted for as existing only partially by virtue of the other three causes advocated by the other three, matters, initiations, and forms. For matters do not account for the nature of the wholes formed from them, initiations of motion can be interrupted and therefore cannot account for their completions, and static forms are unable to explain things in process. The range of completeness in our statement of what things are, therefore, depends completely upon the completeness of the cause by which one identifies 'things,' for causes are themselves derivative. Only by starting with the notion of completion, can the validity of all partialities be acknowledged.

In the same manner, each of the four functions of inquiry, in the effort of each science to make defendable statements about its topic, is subject to greater or less completion of its function as the cause which it uses to guide that function is found to be more or less complete, because of the derivative nature of cause.

(2) *Concerning Interpretation.* Aristotle now turns to the problem of synthesizing these limits, putting them together, to make propositions, statements, for the purpose of indicating what is. But as Aristotle often points out, though a category, or a categorization of something, is something predicated by virtue of something else, simply because we have discovered the kind of thing that is isolable as a candidate for predication, does not mean we have either completed or understood the act of predication. For predication is not understanding, νοῦς, or the abstraction of what exists by virtue of a whole from perception, as discussed in the first Book of the *Metaphysics* and Chapter 19 of Book II of the *Posterior Analytics*. It is rather the act of reason putting two such contents of experience together to form a declaration or attribution about what is. In several places he tells us that a definition is not a statement or argument, λόγος,[8] but may be converted to one. The structure of a predication is not the

8. One of the important differences in nomenclature between Greek and English is that an argument in Greek is not primarily the relation between propositions, but the ratio between a predicate and an underlying topic, for as Aristotle shows in his *Categories*, 1b10, all the properties of the syllogism are simply the implications of what is already contained in attribution or statement, so that both are argument.

structure of a predicate, though one is consequence to the other.

Thus having a definition, we say nothing about the world, although we can turn a definition into an hypothesis by a simple verbal change, thereby changing the function. Not until we make a 'weaving together,' συμπλοκή, bringing limits into a predication, one by virtue of the other, are words and reality connected. For it is not in the entities that the correspondence with reality is touched, but in their interconnection. When this correspondence is accomplished, we discover by the way in which a thinker does this, what his conception of the real is. But interpretation is not itself the problem of determining reality, as some writers have confused the issue.[9] Definitions are unable to implicate reality, for truth and falsity are implicated only in syntheses that implicate fact, and when a procedure of thought does this, it implicates its own notion of the real. It is therefore only at the level of predications that truth and falsity arise, for only at that point in the formation and defense of statement is there a notion of what is real that is implicated. If there is anything different about the notion of reality assumed by a procedure, it shows up in the way the procedure forms predications.

To find 'the why,' διότι, that explains what is 'given' or 'fact,' ὅτι, is not to introduce new existences into the equation. This was Aristotle's great complaint against Plato, for he seemed to populate the world with unnecessary entities. To explicate experience it is not necessary, by Aristotle's procedure, to go beyond the testimony of immediate perception. For those things in immediate experience that are the evidence of themselves, are the evidence also for those that are not. Thus in back of Aristotle's notions of predication there is implied the notion that all of reality is contained within experience, that experience is itself complete, and the problem is to articulate through that cause that will not limit its formulation. Immediate experience leaves us with questions about how things 'given' fit together. They do not

9. See our commentary on the *Metaphysics,* fn. 7, p.16.

make sense as given. Science consists in finding structures between things as 'given' that explain why things are as they appear, making sense of them, without resorting to the fabulous.

Only when two contents at least are related, one to another, is it possible to establish the possibility of a relation between words or thoughts being also a relation between things. Relating words to each other to reflect reality is then the problem of *Concerning Interpretation*. But interpretation is a problem of forming predications, and is not replaceable by a problem about reality, as Walter Watson claimed. There is no such thing as a problem about reality. For different conceptions of reality are simply differences, allowable by the nature of experience to be stated in derivative forms, and implicated in true problems. Different notions of what is real are not simply true or false, but only more or less adequate. The reason there is no problem about reality, no proof about what it is, is that reality, as Kant said of truth, cannot be disputed without being identified, and this is itself the issue. One of the most crucial matters in the comparison of philosophic modes of thought is the determination of what is indeed a problem, for it is not a problem if it cannot be stated independently of any procedure in which it appears. This is why McKeon scoffed at histories of philosophies that talked about Descartes introducing the 'mind-body' problem, for it never was a problem. Rather it was a clash about modes of procedure, not a substantive issue about what is.

The term in Greek for interpretation is ἑρμηνεία, 'hermeneutics,' derived from the name of Hermes, for as both psychopomp for the dead and messenger of the gods he linked psyches to what is the case. One might mythologize the philosophical function by representing the gods as giving their imprimatur to the declarations passing from and to them. For one of the great rewards of the inquiry into language, is the revelation of the perceptiveness of the ancients in their choice of terminology. If modern man could ever understand ancient man's penchant for candidly reporting his deepest thoughts as myths, he might sometimes see there, in those myths, greater wisdom, and more modestly stated, than in his own literal statements.

But since any statement or argument is a predication of one thing 'by virtue of' another, not one thing predicated simply 'of'[10] another, which would be only an accidental connection, any predication at all that is defendable is defendable by being a causal relation between predicate and underlying thing. And therefore all the derivative incompletenesses that we found possible in the formation of categories, are possible as well in the formation of arguments or predications. This results in different theories of interpretation, some of which, just as in determining limits, are more reductive than others.

(3) *The Prior Analytics.* But besides the problems of determining (1) the nature of the 'things' discussed in the various sciences, and (2) the manners of putting these items together to form predications, statements, or attributions about experience, there is then the problem also of (3) linking statements or attributions to each other so as to implicate each other. This is the problem of how one can use established facts in order to justify and validate claims that are not simply factual, but dubious. For as we have said some immediately apprehended attributions are self evident or evident in their being perceived. These then are the principles of the science, either definitions or hypotheses. It is the linkage of these to otherwise dubious attributions that is the problem of method. For the other attributions need evidence external to themselves to be believed. There must then be a way, ὁδός, of showing the dependence of these attributions upon the first or self-evident. To have or be 'with a way,' μέθοδος, then, is

---

10. There is not a single translator of or commentator on Aristotle's logic that has understood how greatly he has destroyed the force of Aristotle's logic by failing to understand this difference. For any predication that is simply 'of' something underlying, is nothing more than accidental. All science is of predications 'by virtue of' what underlies, yet not a single scholar of Aristotle, especially the likes of Ross and Jaeger, has understood this.

not simply to engage in inquiry, as most translations say, but to perceive a cause of the claims one makes in the principles one finds. To have a method is to perceive a cause. And the methods of different procedures are different because the sort of cause to which they appeal is different. The nature of the cause used thus determines method, as well as selection and interpretation.

Method is therefore another dimension to the procedure of any inquiry, distinct from categorizing and interpreting. Method is establishing 'why' this statement is defendable or true on the basis of its relation to statements already known to be true or defendable in themselves. What is common to all methods is the claim that the existence of that conclusion or claim, or the truth of the statement that it exists, is found, at least ultimately, in those principles found existent by virtue of themselves. Method, therefore, has two essential constituents, first that it is the estab-lishment of a hypothetical relation, for a conclusion is true only 'if' that on which it depends is true, and second that the nature of the dependence is a form of 'why,' a claim that the existence of one thing is dependent upon the existence of another, the principle. As Aristotle says many times throughout his scientific writings, that which is offered as 'why' a statement is true is always a cause of the 'being' of the thing stated. But if existence or being is derivative, then things exist in derived and analogous ways, and some will assume that any accident is a scientific statement. For cause is also derivative, and some causes establish the existence of their effects in merely derivative senses, and not their existence completely. And there are four causes of anything. But what has vitiated method the most is the great confusion about the nature of these four causes through bad translation.

The four causes are not distinguished in the *Organon*, but in the substantive writings of Aristotle, like the *Metaphysics* and the *Physics*. Methods, just as categories and interpretations, differ in the cause on which they principally or exclusively depend. For different causes establish their effects in different degrees of completion, τέλος. Whether or not all the causes are available to a method depends on the completeness, τελείωσις, of the cause that rules the method, for some causes allow and necessitate the function of others, some do not. For example, since wholes always have attributes for which the parts give no account, exclusive reliance upon the material cause gives the inquirer no access to attributes dependent upon any of the other causes. The same thing is true of 'that whence the motion,' the initiating cause, or the cause that begins any action, becoming, or process. But 'that whence the motion' was translated by English scholars as the 'efficient' cause, giving the impression that the start of a motion is adequate to its explication. But any motion can 'end' without being 'completed,' and therefore the Greek word end, τελευτή, is sharply distinguished from the word completion, τέλος, as the Greek adjective final, τελευταῖος, is sharply distinguished from the adjective complete, τέλειος. But when Aristotle and Plato were translated by scholars who themselves used derivative methods, they did to Aristotle, Plato, and the Greek language, precisely what their procedures accomplish in accounting for the facts. They made a reductive interpretation of what they said.

The implication of this, if other procedures are partial by restricting themselves to one cause, or at least do not provide for the inclusion of all causes, is that an adequate procedure must then, as Aristotle is constantly advising us, make use of all causes, and do this by starting with the completion of any topic, what he calls 'the being that was,' τὸ τί ἦν εἶναι. For this alone allows inclusion of the others. For as Aristotle argues, *Physics*, 198b2, what is first of all is 'that for the sake of which,' the completion, and the other causes, 198b5, as the matter, that from which, and 'the being that was' or form, are only completed in the substance which is that for the sake of which, so that only the completing cause includes all others. In my first book on Aristotle, *Aristotle's Poetics, Translation and Analysis*, I suggested and then proved that scientific works of Aristotle progress by the successive but separate examination of all the causes that constitute the topic in question. When Aristotle says, as he often does, that another beginning is to be made, he means he is turning to another cause or principle of the topic. The statement made in response by some, asking what was wrong with the first beginning, shows how absurd the interpretations of Aristotle's procedure can be, and how opaque to many are his subtleties.

The point we are now to make is of the greatest scientific and philosophic importance, touching every aspect of any science of any time or state of human knowledge. This we will try to make our definitive statement, since, in discussing logic, we are discussing procedure, where the matter finds its origins.

Method is the use of cause to explain the dependence of one statement upon another. Causes differ in their adequacy in doing this, for one cause being completion, the other three are incomplete in various ways. (1) The material cause explains properties but is incomplete because what structures material always gives it properties it does not possess of itself. (2) The cause which starts the motion is also explanatory, but is incomplete, for being interruptible, cannot account for its own completion. The form explains the properties of the whole, but is unable to account for anything concerning process. A form is a completion of the static. Only what Aristotle calls a completion, τέλος, of a genesis, includes, of its very nature, each of the other three, and therefore this alone attains substance, what exists by virtue of itself, and is the basis of all attributes.

In translating Plato and Aristotle, scholars using reductive procedures, McKeon's structure and discrimination, had no problem with causes expressing the static, matter and form. But they had a great difficulty with the other two causes that deal, not with the static, but the dynamic, things in motion or process. For their translation of Greek was wide of the Greek meaning. For they called the initiating cause 'efficient,' which it is not in the least, since it is interruptible. What Aristotle called 'completion,' τέλος, or 'that for the sake of which,' the completing cause, they falsified even more by calling it the 'final' cause. For τέλος does not mean final, it means complete. The scholars writing for

92

Liddell and Scott made the same reduction of writings that Mill and Kant made of facts. We must take the time to explain this, for the entire understanding of procedure depends upon it.

Using the reductive method that McKeon called the operational method, based exclusively on the initiating cause, mistranslated as 'efficient,' one says an action has an 'end.' Kant's word for this was zwecke, which is the pin or nail that holds up a target at which one aims. But completions cannot be articulated by methods ruled by a reductive cause, which by its nature grasps only a part of the topic. The great dominance of these reductive procedures in western thought, brought about by the Romans, has affected even popular and unsophisticated thought, for indeed we say that in life we have 'ends,' things we attempt to achieve and bring about. But if one thinks for a moment, it is obvious that it is never an 'end' that we seek, even though all completions come at the end. An end or terminus, either in our thinking or in the processes of the world, is never what we want, for a motion or process can be ended before it is fulfilled or completed. What we aim at is always the completion of the thinking or the situation, not their terminus or ending. The operational method is reductive or incomplete because by talking exclusively about beginnings, it is unable to articulate any completion, except as wanted and as making our effort terminated, for completions happen also to be endings. But factually, if we have the method and the cause to grasp it, it is always fulfillment, completion, that satisfies an action, and a completion of itself, necesssarily, includes all, and not only some, of the attributes of the process or motion. Kant talks about a zwecke, and Bentham and Mill talk about ends, but when we read them, we always tacitly supply what they do not atriculate. Because his method relied exclusively on beginnings which are incomplete, Darwin found he had no way of articulating what controlled the process of the formation of new species, and therefore had to say that the determination of the nature of a new species is by chance. For chance, as Aristotle explained, is accusing an acci-

93

dent of being the cause, and wherever in science we find a reference to chance, we should expect the use of a reductive method unable to articulate all the conditions or causes of the fact in question, for chance is the procedural equivalence of ignorance, a restrictive procedure precluding the answer.

The consequences of reductively translating τέλος as end have been catastrophic to the interpretation of Aristotle throughout his works. When he says that nature is a τέλος, as he does in several of his works, the statement has been reductively and sophomorically interpreted to mean that he thought nature had some agenda which it achieved by producing this natural thing. But all he ever meant was that nature, by itself without external influence, (and remember that 'what nature is,' is simply what any substance is of itself, without external influence), affirms its own being, not partially, but completely. He meant that the nature of anything is to be what it is and be that completely. This is factually obvious everywhere. The seeds of things, if not impeded, grow to be precisely the nature latent in the seed, and be it completely. When injured it is the nature of the creature to 'complete' itself, that is, heal itself, not to rest satisfied with an incomplete version of itself. There is no anthropomorphism in Aristotle, no imputation of human 'purpose,' but only that nature is a push to be completely whatever a thing happens to be. The so called 'final' cause is no imposed end, but simply the completion of the substance which defines its function. And the word, which Aristotle explicitly coined to represent this aspect of being, ἐντελέχεια, completeness, was so little understood by the scholars writing Liddell and Scott that they contradicted Aristotle's very statements about it. For a thing exists in ἐντελέχεια, or completeness, not when it exists in 'actuality' or when it is active, as they all said, but when it has completed its generation. A mathematician is still a mathematician when he is asleep. Nor does completeness mean 'absolutely' as they also say. For even the relative exists in completeness when it is completely itself. Such interpretation is what we call reductive, either of reality, or the statements of others about reality. Liddell and Scott are full of such inadequacies, and should be thoroughly rewritten.

As a result the derivative nature of cause, like existence, yields a sequence of explanations from the least complete to the most, with the incomplete being implicit in the complete, because it is implied in its completeness. One needs all four causes to explain the being of anything in experience, though denotatively, two or more causes may be the function of the same thing.

All method grasps what is prior in existence to account for something dependently existent, with all priorities ultimately tracing back to a principle. Any accounting or explaining is the grasp of a cause, and therefore a principle is a cause. The differences lie in the differences in the nature of the cause to which we resort. Both matter and initiation are by nature incomplete explanations of anything, and their contribution is thus only partial. But though form is the grasp of a completion, it is not always the completion of a motion or process. It should be remembered that Plato starts with the assumption that Heracleitus was right, and there is no 'being' in the things that come to be and pass away. He therefore focuses his whole procedure on what abides, the forms imitated or shared by things, and these are the eternal principles of what is. But the forms were never meant to explain process and becoming. That problem is simply bypassed. The relation between being and becoming is put to one side by saying that becoming 'participates in' or 'shares' the forms, but imperfectly, and how this arises is not the problem of knowing. For knowing does not exist in the 'sharing' of the forms, but in avoiding that sharing in the grasp of their perfection.

The sense in which the dialectic method is reductive is not in respect of content, but mode of being. It does indeed grasp completions, but, as assimilation performs the dialectic, they are not the completions that are relevant to the existing world that comes to be and passes away. The only all-encompassing cause is therefore the completion of motion. For only it adequately provides for the contribution of all the other three. But completion is not any reductively interpreted final cause or end, but the fulfillment of any process. For it is only the completion of what it is, its defining function, which any substance, of its own nature, seeks. That completion is the ultimate principle which explains any moving item of experience, by including within its purview the other three conditions of that completion, the matter, the form, and the initiation. For in any area of experience, it is not what is incomplete that explains the complete, but it is the complete, 'the being that was,' that explains the incompletions it requires. Therefore, the primary adage of science is that there must be as much or more reality in the cause, as in the effect.

Method also, therefore, is subject to derivative forms, as in categorizing and interpreting. And again the clue to the derivative or incomplete versions of method is the limitation of the function to only one cause. Thus the method of the physiologists and the atomists, which McKeon called the logistic method, is in fact, though not recognized by McKeon, the reliance solely upon material cause, the implications found between the parts and the wholes that can be compounded from them. For the assumption that this method makes is that everything is explained by the matter of which it is made. Thus they interpret the necessity in a syllogism precisely the reverse of the necessity discussed by Aristotle in his *Prior Analytics*. For the necessity in the syllogism is the need that the conclusion has for the premisses. That is, the conclusion cannot arise without them. But in the logistic or materialistic interpretation of the syllogism, which dominates contemporary textbooks on logic, the necessity is precisely the reverse, for instead of being necessitated by the conclusion, the conclusion is seen as necessitated by the premisses. This indeed is what has led in both psychology and physics to theories of determinism, which betrays the incompletion of their procedure. This derivative version of method, called the logistic by McKeon, though he did not see it was derivative, is found in Newton, Locke, Liebniz, Hobbes, Planck, and in psychology the school of behaviorists like Pavlov, John Watson, and B. F. Skinner.

On the other hand when the method is restricted to the initiating cause, that whence the motion, as in the Greek sophists, Galileo, John Stuart Mill, Darwin, Percy Bridgman, or Stephen Hawking, what McKeon called the operational method, the model is not the deterministic syllogism, but a rhetorical debate. When the method is restricted to the formal cause, as in those using any form of the dialectic, as Plato, Hegel, Marx, Einstein, and Schroedinger, it is the capacity of the more general formula to encompass, explain, and reconcile its contradictory exemplifications that constitutes the linkage of propositions. What Aristotle's procedure aims to show is that the exclusive use of either of the first two explains the complete through the incomplete, which is a reductive fallacy, and that the exclusive use of form alone cannot account for motion.

Thus, in the discussion of the procedure of science there are two major problem areas. First, there is the part we have now covered, (A) the problems relating to the material parts of argumentation, (1) the entities, (2) the predications, and (3) the logical relations between predications, either proof (when only the material cause is used), or persuasion (when only the initating cause is used), or insight (when only the formal cause is used), or finally the resolution of problems (when the completing cause is used). The statement of these logical relations constitute the formulation and explication of fact, and therefore make up most of the content of any scientific treatise. These three factors in inquiry are the topics of the first three treatises of the *Organon*, (1) *The Categories*, (2) *Concerning Interpretation*, and (3) *The Prior Analytics*.

But second, (B) there is the problem of principle on which the whole of science depends, the basis of the truth of reason's predications, and the problems relating to the form of argumentation. There are also three treatises of the *Organon* devoted to this, for just as before there were three 'matters' of argumentation, (1) the things or categories, (2) the statements or predicatings, and (3) the syllogisms or 'arguments together,' so there are

97

three kinds of principles, covered respectively in (4) *The Posterior Analytics*, (5) *On Topics*, and (6) *On Sophistical Refutations*.

It is in the materials of inquiry, (1) the things, (2) the predications, and (3) the implications between predications, that the greatest similarities between various scientific inquiries lie, and the greatest comparabilities can be found. But the forms of inquiry, their nature as a whole, determined by the principle on which they depend, produce the widest differences among inquiries, and most of the problems, the greatest incomparabilities. Of the 184 or so pages in Bekker's Greek text devoted to the *Organon*, 114 are devoted to principles or the form of argument, only 70 pages to the other three, the matters of argument.

There are three kinds of principles covering every conceivable sort of argumentation, valid or invalid. They exhaust the logical possibilities. Principles either are, or are not but only seem to be, what cause something. The *Posterior Analytics* and the *On Topics* discuss arguments based on what is. The *On Sophistical Refutations* discusses arguments that pretend to be based on true principles or on principles that pretend to be true. The *Posterior Analytics* discusses arguments as they are based on what exists intrinsically, because of its own nature. *On Topics* discusses what exists extrinsically, based on the actions or opinions of men.

The heart and soul of Aristotle's logic are contained in these three treatises, for principles most determine what is accomplished. In determining the principle of any science one determines what that existing thing is on which the existence of everything stated about the topic one is investigating depends. Most people suppose that a principle is some generalization, a universal statement pontifically announced with reverence. But Aristotle shows that a principle is an existing thing. For Aristotle's great attack against Plato is that no fatuously hypostatized generalization produces anything, but only an existing thing has the power to produce the object of any science. As he says in both the *Physics* and the *Metaphysics*, generalizations or forms produce nothing. They are only necessary, not sufficient.

98

In the *Posterior Analytics* are contained those matters touching the nature of the principles of the demonstrable sciences, the sciences that rest on the nature of what exists by nature, as these are common to all these sciences, and would be simply assumed within the inquiry of any particular science. In *On Topics* are contained those matters touching, not the nature of what exists by nature, but the most reliable opinions that are themselves constitutive of the topic discussed. In *On Sophistical Refutations* are contained matters touching pretense to truth of any kind.

Within each of the four functions of logic, or the procedural assumotions made by the inquirer to investigate experience, whether that function is (1) categorizing the things to be discussed, or (2) interpreting predications or attributions so as to express the contents of experience, or (3) method, the manner of articulating evidence in support of any predication, or (4) principle, the determination of that existing thing on which the truth and being of what is discussed depends, Aristotle's procedure always takes that stance which incorporates all other possibilites to show that each accomplishes its function, but in an incomplete and reductive fashion, always because the cause used is an incomplete account of existence. These three are the procedures as exemplified by the atomists, the sophists, and the Platonists. But their logically exhaustive character makes them the archi- types of all subsequent thought. What Aristotle says about them is literally applicable to any subsequent example in the history of all thought. As was said at the start, the issues of logic have nothing to do with the historic state of our development or awareness of fact. History shows absolutely no deviation from the procedural possibilities recognized by Aristotle as already established by the Greeks. The incompetence of the procedures that rivaled Aristotle's, either in their works or in modern works repeating them, can be expressed either as a reliance upon a cause that cannot do all they claim it does, or as a reliance on too few causes.

When Richard McKeon developed his brilliant schema of

possibilities which he called 'modes of thought,' it was precisely this same range in the conduct of inquiry as articulated by Aristotle which he also attempted to articulate. But he regarded his four modes, called structure, discrimination, assimilation, and resolution, from the perspective of the mode of discrimination. But as McKeon unconsciously indicated, and as Aristotle consciously showed, this mode is incomplete. As a consequence, McKeon regarded them as four equally valid and comparable manners of inquiry which simply take different and equally valid perspectives on the world. Early in his career in fact he openly stated he was himself using discrimination, but more lately he can be seen to have avoided this identification, without, however, identifying his procedure as being any other.

If, however, he had ever recognized the equivalence between (1) structure and the exclusive reliance upon the material cause, between (2) discrimination and the exclusive use of the initiating cause, between (3) assimilation and the over-arching use of the formal cause, and between (4) resolution and the over-arching use of the completing cause, he would have seen that everything he sought to establish had already been established by Aristotle. For the modes of thought that he so brilliantly distinguished are no different from the various uses of the four causes identified by Aristotle. For the vital factor that McKeon did not recognize, which precluded his identification of his modes with the use of the causes, was that these procedures or modes of thought, instead of being separate and independent perspectives, equally valid and equally justifiable in the perenniel philosophic debate, are in fact derivative procedures, in precisely the sense in which Aristotle said that any topic of greater generality than the categories is derivative, παρώνυμος, analogously related only, and not possessed of the same definition and argument.

Yet it was McKeon himself who laid the basis of this discovery. For it was his genius that saw that for neither structure nor discrimination, that is, neither by the exclusive use of the material or initiating cause, is it possible for there to be any science of the practical. But that there is a procedure which of itself precludes the possibility of science in any area, is enough, by itself, to induicate that the procedure is reductive, or precludes any function possible of procedure generally. It was this fact of their precluding any investigation of the practical, that first suggested to me that McKeon's four modes of thought are not of equal validity or comparable, but that some by their nature are incomplete. But when in 1959 I asked him if his four modes could be compared to the use of different causes, he vigorously denied it twice, only to assume it so in solving a difficult problem in my book the next day.

The basis of all knowing, Aristotle often tells us, is what is complete. This is why neither the material or initiating causes, employed alone, can ever be more than partial explanations of any area of experience. What Aristotle gained from Plato was the insight that the formal cause at least expressed a state of completion, for any form is a whole and its use enables one to recognize, at least in a minimal sense, both the matter and the initiating cause. In the *Timaeus*, for example, both the 'room,' χώρα, and the 'demiurge,' δημιουργής, where the forms are shared, and what produces the sharing, are both given at least a nodding recognition. But nowhere does either Democritus or Protagoras ever recognize the organizing structure of either form or the completion of motion. The use of the formal cause therefore allows in some sense a recognition of matter and initiating push. What Plato especially could not account for in his search for abiding truth, though he saw this no lack, was generation and destruction, motion and change. For that and that alone requires as the over-arching explanation of everything, the notion of completion. That he saw this necessity of procedure, was surely his greatest contribution to knowledge, yet nowhere understood.

The history of thought therefore is a movement from the most simplistic and abstractive, in the sense of being most incomplete, starting with the use of the material cause in the physiologists and atomists, then the insistence upon explaining things,

101

not by their matters, but by their beginnings, the initiating cause, then the recognition that both these approaches are incomplete and what is necessary to explain is the encompassing form that provides stability to be known. Only after these three attempts, abortive because incomplete, came Aristotle's recognition that stable forms unrelated to processes create a world unrelated to what is actually experienced, and what is needed to encompass all these partial views of reality, is the completion of genesis, action, or process. These various procedures advertise their own virtues and vices, for the incomplete must always regard the more complete simply as spurious and invalid, for it is beyond them. The more complete show their greater completion of the scientific quest by their ability to recognize, to various extents, the contributions of the less complete. It is this internal dynamic that precludes the necessity of any ulterior or independent viewpoint from which to judge the competing procedures. For they carry the marks of their validity and adequacy within themselves.

The history of thought thus should culminate in the most comprehensive view, one that is able to articulate the completeness of which all rival procedures are partial fulfillments. But Roman practicalities intervened to reverse the direction of man's thinking. It is the perennial appeal of the simplistic and the opportunistic, however comprehensive man's vision has become, that reverses the process. Nothing illustrates this better today than the popularity in many sectors of the post-modernists whose whole effort is to advocate a reductionist philosophy, and is, of course, simply a return to the procedure of the sophist. Or the popularity of the return to ancient religious failures.

Logic, therefore, is a sort of reflex to the operations of science, somewhat analogous to the way psychology is, to the extent that psychology considers the strictly intellectual faculties of the human. But of course psychology for Aristotle involves more faculties than the intellectual, and there are also the attendant studies, called the *Parva Naturalia*, or the small natural studies, meaning those that study the relation between the soul and

102

the body. For neither psychology nor logic is an investigation of the original phenomena of experience, but if you will, the phenomena of the human's relationship to such phenomena. The writings of a person, therefore, in both psychology and logic, are an intimate view of that human's conception of the conduct of his understanding and reason generally.

The difference between the mind's reflexive view of itself in psychology and in logic is that in psychology the functions are studied without prejudice to the purpose sought, but simply as functions. In logic, on the other hand, the facts of inquiry totally restrict the content of the analysis to the requirements of reason in precisely this function. The entire contents of the six treatises constituting the *Organon* are simply the constituents of successful inquiry, seen under the aegis of Aristotle's more complete mode of thought.

Each of the six parts of logic is examined by Aristotle with an acuity and thoroughness that seems astonishing for its age and time. And with the loss of the writings of those who came before Plato, the works of these two appear as a brilliance that had little or no preparation. And since the thinking of one's predecessors with whom one disagrees is seldom presented as they would present it, even if those predecessors used incomplete procedures, the view of their writings through Plato and Aristotle is not always the most insightful or flattering. Yet giants of the kind of Plato and Aristotle can not have risen without the ground having been well turned before them.

The great virtue of both Plato and Aristotle was that each had a highly reflexive mind, capable of close scrutiny of its own operations, where it is going, and how it is getting there. They were, in other words, men preëminently conscious. For the more complete dialogues of Plato and the organon of Aristotle are reflexive studies of the performance of the mind, par excellence, superbly able to look at itself. This no doubt greatly abetted the survival of their works, for the elimination of error is in great part a function of consciousness.

There are two great issues in the reading of past thinkers. One is the relativity of their factual inquiries to the factual knowledge of their day. The second is the separability of their procedures from the factual content of their inquiries. The proper appreciation of the relativity of factual inquiry to the available facts of the day, is often forgotten or disregarded. For example, some historians of science like to point our that Aristotle, in holding that the earth was the center of the known celestial motions, was in error, while Aristarchus of Samos, born about 64 years after Aristotle, was right in saying that the Sun was the center. But such judgments display a gross misunderstanding of the nature of science and its relation to fact. For there is no divine platform of ultimate truth from which one can pontificate about individual contributions, as such arrogant judges assume. All scientific conclusions are relative to the evidence upon which they are formulated, and truth and falsity are functions of the relation of theories to the facts on which they are based. As paradoxical as it might seem, in terms of the known facts, which is the only standard upon which human judgment can reasonably be based, it was Aristotle who was right and Aristarchus enunciated a theory that was in terms of the available facts totally untenable. For it was Aristotle, not Aristarchus, who was supported by the known facts. Historians who pretend to speak from the perspective of infinite wisdom are the height of the ridiculous. Today's debates, for example, concerning any large and consequential theory must be understood in the same terms. For even if indeed the truth of any theory were to depend only on facts, who will know what facts are needed to finally clarify the issue, and then be able to identify the moment when we have them?

Corollary to this is the problem of the interpretation by modern writers of even the theories of the ancients, so badly do moderns read the ancients. Thus Stephen Hawking lends his prodigious reputation to a totally misconceived identification of the four elements as a misguided 'theory' of Aristotle's. For it was not Aristotle's, but common to all Greeks, nor was it ever a theory, any more than Hawking's (or anyone else's) distinction between Venus and Mars. For the difference between the four elements, does not lie in the difference between fire, air, water, and earth, but between the volatile, the vaporous, the liquid, and the solid, for if ὕδωρ included oil, it certainly did not mean simply water. The elements were not a theory, but a simple classification of things by their perceptible attributes, and this Hawking should have known.

As to the independence of a thinker's procedural assumptions from the tyranny of fact, the ceaseless changes in the procedures of science and philosophy that happen to be in fashion, have the effect of minimizing the tremendous contributions made in the past. For the fact of the separation of procedure from fact is little recognized by all but the greatest thinkers, so that few scientists are able to recognize that objective evaluation of procedure is possible, quite apart from any advance in facts. When all one recognizes is the implication of facts, and there is no awareness of differences in the way such implications can be formed to change procedure, one supposes that past writers, not possessed of the relevant facts, can easily be ignored. All that they have to say of procedure is then tossed aside because of modern ignorance about the nature of procedure. But the only advantage in the flow of the history of science and philosophy is the advance in the techniques of establishing facts. McKeon has shown definitively that there neither has been, nor is there possible, any advance in the range of possibilities in respect of procedures. The Greeks showed that the procedures by which 'facts' are brought to explanation are neither true nor false, but are simply of wider or more narrow ranges of use. They are thus each eternally valid, but each valid only within its own parameters. For validity says little about adequacy to experience, and procedures are therefore narrow or broad, efficient or inefficient, serving different purposes, and such functional matters as are easily comparable. And it is in the comparing of procedures, especially in the writings of the ancients, in which the simplicity of fact makes the nature of procedural difference more obvious, that modern science can learn the most about the validity of its own contributions.

In any comparison of procedures it is the differences in the range of the facts for which they can account which is crucial. But modern science is notorious for neglecting this criterion in favor of precision in results. It is this discounting of the range to which a procedure can be applied, that accounts for the ridiculous identification of what can be scientifically known with what can be measured. The measurable is clearly what is matter, and the criterion reduces science to the most simplistic of all possible objects of study, even by McKeon's account. Second only to this in reductiveness of the scope of science is the criterion that what is scientifically known is the predictable, as in Popper's and James' sophistic view of science. There is a like reduction, but less severe, in Einstein's notion, common to all dialecticians, that ultimate truth lies in the most universal formula, which assumes that what is most real is the rational.

That there is an objective difference between the extent of experience that different procedures are able to articulate, and that precision, predictibility, and universality are all reductive of what is most complete, completeness of being, is the supreme lesson of Aristotle's logic. Thus McKeon's schema, so beautifully articulating procedures on Aristotle's schema, must be severely amended to show that procedures are, not equally acceptible views of the world, the sophist's view, but derivative precisely as cause is derivative, comprehended in the one that is most substantial. For the contributions of different procedures is nowhere more visibly seen than in their having, or not, the capacity to view other procedures as part of their own requirements of science. The procedure that sees no place for its rival does so from the narrowness of its view. The most complete is the most accepting. And the degree of completion is determined by the cause on which it depends.

COMMENTARY ON

ARISTOTLE'S *CATEGORIES*

Chapter 1. More often than convenient for readers, Aristotle makes statements or distinctions, simply for the record, without indicating their purpose. This fact alone shows how ridiculous is the claim that these are his lecture notes for teaching. He is not writing for others, but recording for himself what is crucial of his thinking. Often it is for the reader, then, to worry out the whys of what he says, and this occasions disputes about his meanings.

The treatise starts by distinguishing three attributes given things when the soul 'states' things by making predications or arguments. If things are stated homonymous, i.e. if different sorts of things are named the same, syllogism is impossible, for the name is ambiguous. To 'state,' then, is to affirm something to be something, as predicating X of Y, and λέγω is not used of making a prayer or reading a poem. However, Greek scholars have not shown themselves sensitive to such nuances of the Greek. If the things or 'limits,' ὅροι, as later treatises call the ultimate parts of argument, are synonymous, 'named together,' the arguments can be demonstrative, but if derivative, only dialectical. 'Things' are the 'limits' of the analysis of inquiry into its functional parts, syllogism, argument, and limit. Aristotle's logic is not about words, but about the procedure by which 'things' can be known.

The verb λέγεται, 'to state,' illustrates the fact that the logical, ἡ λογική is what is required in order for the inquirer, or 'subject,' to successfully 'state' facts about 'objects.' Even lexicons tell us that *Categories* should be translated 'predicatings' or 'accusations,' for in 'stating' anything we are 'accusing' a thing experienced of 'existing' in a certain way. The title of this treatise is thus more properly *Predicatings*, than *Categories*, for a κατη-γορία is an act of the subject, not an object that a subject finds already classified. Much less is a category a 'term,' for science determines the nature of things, not words, and obviously it is not names that are similarly or derivatively named, but things. Yet, in the name of modern fashion, translators go through verbal gymnastics in changing the Greek to make Aristotle speak of linguistic entities when the Greek speaks simply of things.

What is predicated, τὸ κατηγόρημα, the 'thing stated,' as opposed to the act of predicating or accusing, does not answer "What kinds of things are found in our experience," but the far more subtle question "of what sorts do we say are the things of which we make statements or predications." 'Things stated' thus are not simply found in experience, but formulated through some procedure of thought or reason, in stating predicates. Things stated, τῶν λεγομένων, are thus the things referred to in speech. But because in our semantic custom 'what is stated' is either the 'things' that words refer to, or the 'words' that refer to things, the ambiguity of English is thought to allow a translator to turn Greek metaphysical statements into semantic statements to accord with modern fashion. When the discussion consciously turns to a different problem in *Concerning Interpretation*, it will then speak of verbal matters, an 'expression,' ῥῆμα, stated of a 'name,' ὄνομα. But categorizing is formulating, by one's own thought processes, the things of which one speaks.

The opening, then, says that 'things' are named the same in three ways, homonymously, when the things have different arguments[1] made of them, synonymously, when the arguments or statements are the same, and derivatively or paronynously (besides the name) when the thing exists in various analogous ways

---

1. In English an argument is a syllogism, because in modern reductive logic what connects a statement does not connect a syllogism. But since, as 1b10 says, syllogism is based on predication, in Greek an argument is any predication, as at 4a36 "someone is sitting" is an argument. Thus λόγος is not 'definition,' ὁρισμός, as in other translations.

in relation to one fundamental form of the thing. The paragraph is thus talking about how, though things may have the same name, the arguments made of them can be either different, the same, or analogous. There are times in the *Organon* when he talks of the elements of speech, but not here. For part of the problem of inquiry is that of 'stating' things, through relating things, thoughts, and words, so that words signify thoughts and thoughts signify things. But translators should not use this happenstance to turn metaphysical statements about wxisting things, into semantic statements about words.

Thus, 'things,' or the entities of which science speaks, are not simply 'given' to experience, as assumed by simplistic procedures that say all we need are facts, as for example A. J. Ayer. Things are themselves the products, or at least the implications, of the way inquiry formulates them. For initially inquiry has no ready-made 'objects.' Of the four functions of thought, all already distinguished by Aristotle, McKeon's 'selection' is what Aristotle called categorizing, the determination of the 'things' that arguments are about. For statements cannot be formulated without first distinguishing the things related in predications, just as predications must be formulated prior to syllogisms. And since, as Aristotle saw, but McKeon did not, a scientific predication is always the determination of a cause, how things are categorized is a matter of the nature of the cause used in doing so.

Because these are only his private notes to himself, Aristotle does not state the reason here in Chapter 1, but the things 'stated' must be distinguished into these three sorts, homonymous, synonymous, or derivative, because this is crucial in understanding the different problems of stating encountered in different kinds of inquiries. For both when one demonstrates and when one argues dialectically one must understand of which sort is the topic discussed. In physics and biology the things demonstrated are synonymous, while in politics and ethics they are only derivative things, and in metaphysics too, what is discussed is necessarily derivative in nature.

Things that are homonymous, or 'named the same,' but of which the arguments, λόγοι,[2] are not the same, but 'other,'[3] are things of which there is no science. For demonstrative science needs things always to be synonymous, 'named together,' so as to have the same thing in every argument, which in our semantic age we call having the same meaning. But paronymous things, or things named besides, only analogously the same, have arguments which are also analogous only and not literally the same. Things named in this way are still capable of syllogism, but not demonstrative syllogism. Medicine talks about doctors, drugs, and therapeutic procedures, all of which are medical or related to health, but analogously, and not accidentally, by all relating to one thing that is fundamentally medical or healthy, the body. Thus penicillin is medical or healthy, but not as an operation is, or as a doctor is. And the analogues are all some manner in which 'the medical' or 'the healthy' exists. For each of these is a condition or cause by which 'the healthy' exists. They are either the things 'which,' or 'from which,' or 'by which,' or 'to which' the healthy either is or comes to be, which are the causes of the being of the healthy. Thus also justice in an oligarchy is only an analogue to justice in a democracy, so that political science talks analogically of justice. Practical science thus uses derivative limits. Things are derivative when the primary function exists more or less completely, either because it consists of various contributing factors (causes), or because it exists in various incomplete forms (through the omission or partiality of a cause). The naturally partial analogues are indicated in an inflected language like Greek by inflections, and in positional languages like English by qualifying phrases. In practical science the causes are then analogically related in the science, but contemplative science separates them.

2. See fn.1, p.108.
3. On the difference between different, διάφορος, as having another form, and other, ἕτερος, or ἄλλος, as things are numerically other while not being different by having the same form, see p. xvi.

The difference between the three ways of being named the same is fundamental in discussing the 'what,' the topic, or the limit, of any scientific argument. Yet commentaries seem to find no use for the distinction. The demonstrative sciences like *On Natural Things*, the *Parts of Animals*, and *On the Soul* speak of synonymous things. For reasons determined by differing circumstances, the *Metaphysics*, and such sciences as the *Nicomachean Ethics*, the *Politics*, and the *Art of Rhetoric*, as well as the arguments establishing principle in any science, state derivative things.

Chapter 2. By things stated, τῶν λεγομένων, the Greeks meant the things referred to, not the words that do this. To refer to the speaking of words they would use the verb 'express,' ἐρῶ, or 'say,' φημί, which focus on the subject, not the object. Some things stated are stated by virtue of being woven together (and are then complex), some are not (and are then simple). Aristotle is not speaking of verbal simplicity and complexity, but of 'things' that are simple or complex. 'The man standing by the fence' is verbally complex, but the thing is one and simple, as he says is 'human,' and 'runs.' The difference, therefore, is that between things as catergorized and things as woven together into statements or predications to be interpreted. This distinction separates the topics of these two treatises. For what is not woven together, as 'ox' and 'wins,' are things to be categorized, or whose state of being is distinguished in the *Categories*, while things woven together, as 'human runs' or 'human wins,' are things interpreted, or related to fact, according to considerations developed in *On Interpretation*. Aristotle assumes that if 'human runs' is true, the weaving together of 'human' and 'runs' is an objectly existing thing. Our culture is so obsessed with semantics, that this insight is lost. Understanding, νοῦς, is what grasps things in their unwoven state. Reason or argument, λόγος, weaves them together, existingly or not.

At 1a20 he changes from 'things as stated' to 'things as existing' to distinguish between two ways of existing by virtue of interweaving. For in one way things are interwoven by one thing (the predicate) being stated 'by virtue of' the thing underlying (the predicated). In other words, the connection between predicate and underlying thing lies in the existence of the underlying thing being the cause of the existence of the predicate. In the other way, one thing is stated to be 'in' the underlying, but not as a part. For a thought is in the soul, and color is in a body, not as a tooth or muscle is in a body, by being a part of it, but as being unable to exist without the existence of that in which it is. That is, the attribute in this case has an existence dependent upon what underlies, but not caused by it.

This is a distinction that is totally obtuse to modern textbooks on logic, because it is impossible for reductive procedures to articulate either predications existing 'by virtue of' what underlies, or predications stating existential dependence. This is why they use Venn diagrams, for these clearly substitute class inclusion for both causal relations and existential dependence. The preposition κατά·is not correctly translated in either the Oxford or the Loeb.[5] For a predicate existing 'by virtue of' what underlies is not stated 'of' that thing, as these both say, but exists 'because of' what underlies. For an accident is predicated 'of' something, as 'the horse is chestnut' or 'the horse is running up the hill,' but four legged and animal are predicated, not simply 'of' the horse, but 'by virtue of' or 'because' it is a horse. The difference is incomprehensible to anyone who thinks Hume accomplished anything significant for science[6] or who thinks scientific or logical relations can be signified by Venn diagrams.

It is only what is predicated 'by virtue of' what underlies that is the basis of science, and without which there is no science. But not a single translator of Aristotle ever understood the Greek well enough to translate the word κατά correctly.[7] In the other case, being attributed to something as we attribute a

5. Cf. our comments p.xv.

6. For those thinking Hume's criticism of cause significant, I have elsewhere shown that Aristotle foretold and answered every criticism.

112

thought to a person, or color to an object, the predicate is not attributed by virtue of what underlies, but is simply designated to be dependent, that is, of uncaused, but accidental existence. And such a relation, of course, is the basis of no science.

When the difference between existing by virtue of something, and simply existing in something, is understood, it is possible to make some fine distinctions, for (1) the forms of substances exist by virtue of the individual existing, but do not exist in them, else they would not exist in another. (2) Color exists in a body but not by virtue of anything, else the predication would be demonstrable. (3) Science not only exists in the soul but also by virtue of the grammatical. Finally, (4) some things, like individual substances, a horse or human, exist neither in something nor by virtue of something. Thus the things that exist primarily are (4), individual substances, which suffer neither of these dependence of existence, and are therefore the basis of all science. The things that science is able to demonstrate on their basis are (1) and (3), because they exist by virtue of substance, but in different ways, while (2) is totally accidental.

To effect these distinctions the proper translation of κατά is thus imperative. At 1a28 Aristotle says "color is stated by virtue of nothing underlying," but at 2a31 he says "white is predicated of the underlying body." This obviously becomes a contradiction when the translator sees no difference between the two, and the result is either panic, if you perceive it, or bliss if you don't.[8] Aristotle omits κατά precisely at those points in which the predi-

7. The error is immense. In the first four chapters Aristotle uses the word κατά, 'by virtue of,' no less than 33 times. In Chapter 5 he uses it 30 times, and 71 times in the whole treatise. On not a single occasion was it correctly translated either by E. M. Edghill, J. L. Akrill, Jonathan Barnes, or H. P. Cooke. In the whole of the *Categories*, against these 71 times, the phrase properly translated 'predicated of' is used only 9 times, 1b22, 2a21, 29, 30, 32, 3a16, 28, 12a7, and 16. This crucial basis of all science was completely obscured by bad translation. Even Liddell and Scott badly stated κατά.

cation is merely statistical, an accident, and not a scientific predication. It is the difference stated best in the *Posterior Analytics*
between things that are merely true and therefore at times defea-
sible, and things that are necessary. But the correct translation is
obvious if it is pointed out that everywhere Aristotle says science
is the grasp of cause, so only predicates 'by virtue of' what underlies are scientific. The profusion of such mistakes, as I have
often said, is due to the dominance since Roman times of the
reductive procedures, especially the strict reliance on the material
and initiating causes, for whom Aristotle is an enigma.

The thing that is so significant about these distinctions laid
down by Aristotle is that he is stating the defining charateristic of
any topic of science, and no one translating Aristotle before this,
not even students of McKeon like Apostle, has understood this.
For McKeon himself never understood that the modes of
thought are based on cause. Only what exists 'by virtue of' something else can be demonstrated. All else is either a part of analytical understanding, contributive of the facts on which science is
based, or totally accidental to science. It means therefore that
every statement demonstrated in any science is the statement of a
cause, or contributes to a cause. It states what exists by virtue of
a topic, such as its matter or parts, its source of motion, its
structure or formula, or the fulfillment of its function, as I first
stated in my book on the *Poetics*. The variation between procedures, their derivative natures, is totally dependent on the inclusiveness of the cause one has chosen to govern one's procedure.
For cause, as in the above examples, is a derivative thing, being
all by itself the basis of the inclusion or exclusion of facts.

8. To obscure from the reader the contradiction he had produced
Edghill arbitrarily changed the verb in the statement at 2a31 to 'a body
is called white.' But Aristotle's distinction remained unrecognized. This
is deviousness to cover up confusion. Ackrill and Barnes were even
more duplicitous by simply excising whatever they did not understand,
and claiming falsely that everyone else does it. Harold P. Cooke (Loeb)
simply never noticed he had produced a contradiction.

All scientific statements are statements about the causes of the topic at hand, because to explain anything is to show the source of its being, and that upon which anything depends is its cause. When men think metaphysically, i.e. assume the primary scientific task is determine 'what is,' they are therefore less likely to be led astray by alien concerns. But when philosophy turns to epistemology or semantics, i.e. either 'how one knows' or 'what is meant,' the possibility of loosing sight of the goal of science is immense. For it is more than likely that in epistemology one becomes satisfied with merely how propositions are dependently related on one another, for that is what epistemolgy does, and in semantics it is more than likely that one becomes satisfied with merely the interpretation of things, for that is what semantics does. But as we have shown, complete inquiry needs not only (1) the selection of things, (2) the interpretation of predications, and (3) the method of relating propositions. It also needs to determine as well (4) the principles on which the entire argument is based, and in a metaphysical approach it is impossible to forget that science proves the existence of things.

The ease with which one in science looses sight of the fact that the task of science is to determine the priorities between the 'being' of things is shown in the reductive interpretation of syllogistic reasoning through Venn diagrams. For Venn diagrams reduce all science to class inclusion, which has absolutely nothing to do with the dependence of the existence of one thing upon another. When the logical arguments of science are equated to the chance relations revealed in Venn diagrams, logical texts have lost all connection with the task of science. The whole of Lord Russell's work, whether his own *Principles of Mathematics*, or his joint effort with Alfred North Whitehead, show this trivialization of logic, making it irrelevant to the task of science which is to explain facts. The whole notion of science as based on statistics shows the same inability to see that science searches, when it is complete, for priorities in existence, not accidental relations, for only existences explain existents, nor correlations. Statistics are facts only, not whys, but what is worse, when at the start there is no awareness of the difference between accidental and essential connections, the very possibility of science disappears. Logical arguments are built on predication, not predications 'of,' but predications 'by virtue of,' and only so do predications show the being of one thing dependent on another, not on things being 'contained' within each other, or having other accidental relations to each other. For the sophistical manner of categorizing accepts ostensive rather than functional notions of a class, as Russell's class of red things, extrinsic relations, which cannot be the predication 'by virtue of' the thing underlying stating a dependence of being. Yet verbally both relations are stated by the same words. As 'snow is frozen water' states a predicate by virtue of the nature of snow. 'Snow is white' says only that 'what is white' is in the snow, not that 'what is white' is predicated by virtue of the snow. For, as Aristotle says, every color is in a body, but never stated by virtue of what underlies. It is also not by virtue of its being snow that it is white, because other things are also white.

The problem of the *Categories*, then, is that of determining the nature of the ultimate limits of inquiry, the entities, τὰ ὄντα, about which statements, predications, or arguments are made and into which they divide. There is obviously a connection between our accustomed speech concerning existing things and the requirements of logic, but logic is not a description of *de facto* language, for customary speech may or may not be in every respect suitable for the requirements of science. And it is obvious that there are practicalities to common speech that are inimicable or irrelevant to what science requires. The language of logic is thus derivative as the procedures of science are derivative, by virtue of the completeness of the cause that the inquirer seeks.

Chapter 3. As we said, the verb λέγω, to state, is the common way of referring to speech as it refers to an object. The verb κατηγορέω, to predicate or categorize, to which he now changes, more consciously draws attention to this function. Aristotle's change from 'state' to 'predicate' is a sign of his regard for logic as a precise articulation of one natural function of speech, the solutions of problems. And the verb 'to categorize,' meaning to classify, or to indicate the kind, is not so far a change from the original meaning, 'to accuse of being.' It is part of the adjustment of 'stating,' from inexact practicalities of everyday life, to the rigors needed for stating one knows.

But this relation of predication, when properly understood and not as reductive translation has understood it, is stated to be transitive. For whenever something is predicated by virtue of what underlies, whatever is predicated by virtue of what is predicated, is also predicated by virtue of what underlies. He explicitly does not say, as every previous translator has made him say, that whatever is predicate 'of' what is predicated, is also predicated 'of' what underlies. For this translation is completely false. What is predicated 'of' something is not at all transitive. If corn is yellow and yellow is a color, any fool knows that it does not follow that corn is a color, except, of course, those who translated Aristotle without thinking. There is only one other topic whose careless and incompetent translation has had such egregious and palpably harmful consequences.[9] How could one with a modicum of intelligence have possibly translated Aristotle in this way without seeing they were speaking nonsense? If one is playing baseball, and playing baseball is a game, is one then oneself a game?

All demonstrative science depends upon this transitive relation. When B is attributed to A by virtue of A, it means that the nature of A is the reason for the predication of B, and when the nature of B is also the cause of C, it then follows that the nature of A is also the cause of C. There is therefore no relation contained in the syllogism that is not contained in the predication, and if a syllogism is an argument, it is only because a predication is an argument. It was only when Rome taught the west how to be sophistical that while the syllogism remained an argument, the predication ceased to be one, because the whole relation between

9. That concerning τέλος.

117

premisses and conclusion changed. For inclusion in a class, as used by Russell, has nothing to with predication or science.

For example, by Aristotle's account the function of the syllogism is the formulation of the cause by which a predicate is attributed by virtue of what underlies, it does not necessitate a particular instance of the connection, for anything might intervene. The necessity involved is the necessity of the premisses for the existence of the conclusion. But reductive logic makes the conclusion necessary on the basis of the premisses, and then gets into the problem whether universals involve existence, because that necessity is fortuitous. Such procedures, as in behavioristic psychology, then get committed to nonsense like determinism.

The two paragraphs of chapter 3 are devoted respectively to the predication first of genus and then of difference. In the case of differences, it is only when the things underlying are ordered under one another, as monkey is under primate, that the differences are transitive. The clarification of the function of genus and difference in predication is obviously of importance, since it is genus and difference that make up the parts of definition.

Chapter 4. The first three chapters sort out the distinctions that make possible the distinction between the categories, or the 'limits' of the analysis of inquiry into its logical parts. If the earlier distinctions came out of a contemplation of experience, these do even more emphatically. Previous translations uniformly call them linguistic entities, words or expressions, but a category is rather an existing thing, a manner of being, that is represented by a word, and to be represented by a word is not to be a word. The Greek τῶν εἰρημένων, 'things expressed,' unlike τῶν λεγομένων, ambiguously means either the objects referred to or the expressing or stating words, but throughout it is clear that Aristotle calls them things, and only at times words.

In various works Aristotle lists the categories in various numbers. Here he lists as many as he ever does, 10, but there is never a statement that any list is complete, but each list is made according to the problem being considered. They are therefore experientially derived, not distinguished logically, but, as we have just said, it is only within a given science that any instance is determined to be of a kind.

The translations of these categories are more difficult than the ideas expressed. They are all said to be not complex or woven together by reason, and therefore simple, and, as the ultimate entities, or limits of statement in arguments, cannot be further analyzed into parts. They are the highest order of differentiation applicable to 'that which is.' That is, they are the highest order of synonymous existence, since anything that exists by virtue of a greater whole exists only paronymously, or derivatively, by virtue of analogy. Or to put the matter into contemporary idiom, erroneously assuming them terms, the categories are terms of the highest order of univocality. For to say that each category exists, is to use the word exist analogically, not univocally.

Translators have been concerned to render all these as nouns, but we think them most accurately stated as Aristotle did. For he gave only one anything close to a noun, the first, and that is a noun only by transformation of a verb, for it is essentially a participle. The second and third are interrogative adjectives, the fourth is a phrase, the fifth and sixth are interrogative adverbs, and the last four are all infinitives, the seventh being passive, the last three active. Apparently clarity of expression was more important to Aristotle than our modern desire for uniformity of nomenclature, for translators have thought linguistic uniformity more important than accuracy. For though Greek allows such uniformity, Aristotle does not avail himself of it here, as in other matters he frequently does. They have the form they have so they can be seen as normal expressions for the kinds of 'existing' that he is concerned to distinguish. The traits of English usage are quite parallel, and these parallels should be used rather than substantives which produce superficial neatness. It is as though Aristotle is saying only the substantive is substantive, and therefore his nomenclature is self-descriptive. What is expressly to be noted is that Aristotle is very concerned that, whatever precision

119

of language he develops, it always rises out a common sense language which serves as basis. Science is not opposed to common sense, but its clarification.

Most categories are clear enough, save the seventh and eighth. The seventh, κεῖσθαι, has been translated 'position' and 'posture,' the eighth, ἔχειν, as 'state.' In Greek the seventh category is the passive infinitive of the verb to lie or be laid. Greek infinitives are regularly translated by English participles when they are used substantively, with articles, as in these cases. For the seventh we have used the participial phrase 'being situated,' because the noun 'position' is too ambiguous, for it can refer to relation (third from the left), and 'posture' is also ambiguous, for it can refer to attitude which would be the eighth category, etc.

The eighth category is the active infinitive of the verb to have or possess, ἔχει, and remembering that a habit comes from that very root, both in English and in Greek, and that in common parlance a dress and a virtue are equally habits, we should keep in mind that a virtue is what we 'have,' a habit, ἕξις, as a way of deporting ourselves, or functioning, not a passive 'state' we are in, as in the word 'static,' which is merely a being affected, not a way of doing. 'State,' therefore, is a very misleading translation, both here and in the ethics. The issue will return in chapter 15. For this category we have used the participle 'possessing.' Our own translations are based as much on Aristotle's use of these terms through the rest of his works as the examples he gives here. For example, the fact that a glass holds half a pint is said by Aristotle to be something it possesses, and the shirt on one's back is said to be a having or possession, but it is a sophomoric misunderstanding of the Greek to call these 'states' of the thing that possesses them, for neither courage nor a shirt can reasonably be called a state.

Chapter 5. If science is 'stating something by virtue of something else,' it implies a priority in existence among 'things stated,' which as we have said is the vital factor missing in reductive notions of logic such as guide modern text-books. For that by virtue of which anything is stated must be prior in being to anything stated 'by virtue of' it. But this does not hold of things stated simply 'of' another thing. One does not explain anything through its consequences. Again, if κατά is translated 'of,' as has been the universal custom, and not 'by virtue of,' the whole point is lost. And just as at 1b10 'predication of' something is not transitive, while 'predication by virtue of' something is transitive, so also this implication of priority does not hold if something is merely stated 'of' something else. For when predication is interpreted merely as class inclusion, all notion of priority of being is lost. The translations then must be exact if we are to understand what Aristotle is doing.

But neither the transitive relation of predication nor the relation of priority is infinite, but there must be that which is not only prior, but first, i.e. that by virtue of which other things are stated, but not itself stated by virtue of anything else. It is prior existentially or in the sense that whatever is stated by virtue of it depends upon it for its existence. The name we customarily give to such independence of existence, on which the existence of all else depends, is substance. The chapter thus starts by saying, of all 'things stated,' substance is neither stated as 'existing in' something else, nor stated 'by virtue of' something else. For if it existed 'in' anything else or was predicated by virtue of anything else, that other thing would have prior existence. This is why in every science the first thing to be determined is that 'thing' in that problematic area on whose existence, as substance, all other attributes depends. And showing that dependence constitutes the demonstrations that make up the science.

Other things, then, are stated only by virtue of the priority of substance. The priority of substance of which Aristotle is speaking here, then, is a priority of predication in the statements about what exists, taking something from the flow of experience and applying it to an identified locus, affirming in that predication either the simple or partial existence of the underlying thing. Thus the priority of substance is necessitated by the very nature of our 'stating' anything. As we have said, Aristotle's term for substance, οὐσία, is a substantiation of the feminine participle of the verb 'to be,' and has a long history as a term referring to reality or what is. It was not coined by Aristotle, though no one else used it with his sweeping ramifications.

At 2a11 Aristotle brings out three criteria of priority in the act of predicating; commandingly, κυρίως, primarily, πρώτως, and mostly, and in all three senses of prior, substance, in the sense of the individual thing, a certain man or horse, is prior in existence because it is presupposed in predication. The word 'commandingly,' κυρίως, comes from κυρόω which means to establish, master, determine, validate. The name of Cyrus, the founder of the Persian empire, is cognate to it. The thing that is commanding settles things, as an author settles things in his book, as a magistrate settles things in the court. In this case, substance establishes the existence of everything else. 'Primarily' means first, either in the order of being or time. 'Mostly' means there is more existence in substance than in the things it causes to exist, for a dependence in being is less being, as what makes things hot is hotter than the things it makes hot. Any cause is more real than that which it causes, and in seeking the cause of fact, science is the search, in any area of fact, for what is more real. Its arguments, then, start from what is most real, not from the things first grasped as real.

Substance, in the sense of the individual thing, is alone of things in experience self-subsistent, existing by virtue of itself. All other 'things' exist by being dependent upon primary substance, and therefore exist in a derivative way, just as all the incomplete causes, such as matter, initiation, and form. At 2a14, the form of the individual thing is secondarily substance, because the individual thing is attributed to that form. Form is not species for a species is form and matter, and form is proper to the individual while genus is common to many. In the same way higher genera, even further removed, are attributed. For forms are predicated by virtue of the 'whole together,' matter and form, while genera are predicated by virtue of forms. So too, the *differentiae* or differences between members of the same genus. These are existences existing 'by virtue of a whole,' not individual things. In contemporary biological taxonomy these distinctions are all handled sophistically like Russell's class of red things, as simply an arbitrary naming of enumerated groups of greater inclusiveness, with no functional difference. But Aristotle saw a difference in kind between a structure that was the form of an existent, and a structure that was a 'form of a form.' Modern biology, under the influence of biologists like Darwin who used the method of the sophists, treats species, genus, families, classes, phylla, etc., all nominally, like counters, without functional distinctions. So also mathematicians today treat the unit sophistically as itself a number, not as the measure of number with number as the counting of the units. Modern science, dominated by the sophistical and materialistic procedures against which Aristotle struggled in all his works, treats everything 'stated by virtue of a whole' statistically and all as one sort, and therefore cannot distinguish what is attributed to all and to all as such.

At 2a19 he shows the importance of what is stated 'by virtue of' what underlies, versus what is stated 'of' what underlies. For in the first case, but not in the second, it is necessary that both the name of that predicate and any argument (predication)[10] stated by virtue of that predicate are also predicated 'of' that underlying thing. Again, notice that the predication 'of' the name and argument depend in such a case, not on a prior predication 'of,' but a prior predication 'by virtue of.' But, as indicated above, this cannot be seen in other translations.

Without predication being transitive there is no way of using one predication to establish another in reasoning, and the whole of science becomes impossible, except the sophistic way of

10. If λόγος is translated 'definition,' simply because 'it works,' all predicates by virtue of the thing itself, not a part of the definition, are excluded. Aristotle never uses argument, λόγος, for 'definition.'

making predication simply class inclusion. For there is no way of knowing that a predication is necessary unless it is the very nature of the underlying thing that justifies the predication of it. Or to show the analytic character of the method of logic, the entire theory of the syllogism is analytically derived from the notion of one thing being predicated 'by virtue of' another. Again, this shows dramatically the importance of correctly translating the preposition κατά, for there is no science when the predication is simply 'of' something else. Again Aristotle talks about things, and only secondarily words, for it is 'things' to which names are predicated, so that the entire discussion of what is now known as 'entailment' and about language, must, for Aristotle more complete account, be existential, not nominal. It therefore follows that the entire theory of the syllogism follows from Aristotle's approach to inquiry as a relation between subject and object which focuses on existence through reason's act of predication, the act of the observer in forming unities of experience.

At 2a27 it is shown that the preceding does not hold in most cases of things 'existing in' something, for most times neither the name nor the argument of what exists in something is stated of it. Sometimes the name is stated of it, but never the argument. For example, if what is white exists in a body, the body is stated to be white, but any argument, including its definition, concerning what is white is not predicated by virtue of the body. Back at 1a28 this was stated of color generally, but translators did not notice, for they had not distinguished what is predicated merely 'of' something, and 'by virtue of' something.

There are several matters here that need greater attention than given so far. Aristotle uses the term form, εἶδος, not for the infima species, but for its form, and things of the same form are numerically 'other,' but not different. We may remember that for Aristotle matter is the principle of individuation. The term genus γένος, or kind, refers to any higher order of what exists by virtue of a whole, in which being other might also include being different. Thus, though two robins are only 'other,' a sparrow and a

124

robin are 'different.' The term διάφορον, difference, refers to form, which distinguishes one sort from another within a higher sort. Within species things are only 'other,' ἕτερος or ἄλλος, with no difference in form, while between genera things are 'different,' διάφορος, or other in form. This is another of Aristotle's distinctions universally ignored in translation. All of these, forms, genera, and differences, exist 'by virtue of a whole,' that is, each exists because it is the nature of individuals as a whole.

The distinction between what exists simply 'by virtue of all' and what exists 'by virtue of a whole' is crucial to science, as Aristotle says in the *Posterior Analytics*, 73a28 and 73b26. But in English the word 'universal' does not convey the notion of a whole, as a check of almost any dictionary will show, even though it did in Latin, for it expresses only the notion of 'all.' That is to say, to say something is true of all of a certain group however specified, is a merely statistical matter, if it does not say the predication exists functionally, 'by virtue of a whole' or 'as such,' or by virtue of that group, as a group, having a certain form. The κατά, 'by virtue of,' therefore, in καθόλου, is ignored when the latter is translated 'universal,' and what is essential is turned into an accidental statement. Thus in English one would naturally say it is universally true that all isosceles triangles are equal to two right angles. But Aristotle denies this by pointing out that this predication is not καθόλου to isosceles, because it is triangle on the whole that has this property. This is why it is unqualifiedly false to translate καθόλου as universal. This turning of Aristotle's functional logic at crucial points into modern statistical logic modeled on and reproducing the sophistical logic of Aristotle's day has been avoided by no translator to date, and this error, and others of the kind, have falsified Aristotle's statements.

We know at this point that Aristotle is not a 'nominalist,' holding that what exists by virtue of a whole are simply words referring to no reality. For predicates such as forms, genera and differences are real, though existing differently from concrete things. They exist as 'things stated by virtue of a whole' are wont to exist, and this is the way their existence is expressed.

The word λόγος, or 'argument,' may refer either to the existential 'thing,' the ratio or proportion between a predicate and something underlying, the thought of this, or the statement of the thought or existential relation. That is, an argument is either a relationship between existential entities, or the faculty (reason) that grasps that relation, or the speech that states that existential or ideational relation. For often Greek uses the same word for thing, thought (faculty) or word, for at the optimum, where there is a thing, there is a corresponding thought and a word to refer to both. But Aristotle always uses the name of the thing he means, a genus when that is meant, the form when that is meant. There are no cases in which he uses terms incorrectly as implied by translating λόγος as definition, a form for a genus. For this would be like using monkey for a mammal.

The argument always given for translating the same Greek term with many English words has been that the Greek word has many meanings. But this is the sheerest sophistry. It is not that the Greek has many meanings, but that the English word one has chosen is now proven inadequate. Only a sophist would turn a statement about the inadequacy of his own choice into false accusations about the variability of Greek. But there is a word in English that quite adequately approximates the Greek λόγος, if we understand by argument not only a relationship between two words or thoughts, but also the things so signified, in each case either as activity or as power. For then 'argument' is equally a faculty of the soul, a form of things, or a verbal structure.

As we showed in the commentary on the *Nicomachean Ethics*, argument or reason, λόγος, is the faculty that makes connections, as opposed to the understanding, νοῦς, which grasps the original intellectual contents from experience. Any assertion, therefore, between a predicate and something underlying is an argument or act of reason, the grasp of a ratio or proportion between two contents of the understanding, not a definition. A definition, ὁρισμός, Aristotle tells us in the *Posterior Analytics* at

126

72a18, is a thesis, either part of a contradiction, that simply leaves out the predication of existence, stating 'what' without stating 'that.' If the notion of existence is brought in, making a claim that the thing exists, it becomes an hypothesis, a claim of reason. It is therefore not the notion of existence that turns mere speech φάσις, into argument, but proportion, ratio, relationship, between things understood, as well as thoughts and words so signifying.

The term φάσις, incidentally, Liddell and Scott incorrectly call assertion, while Aristotle assures us at 17a17 that assertion is only an accident of φάσις, for name and expression, he there says, are only speech, φάσις, and not yet declaration ἀπόφανσις. Liddell and Scott have been confused by the fact that, as in English, the word speech is used of declarations, so even Aristotle uses φάσις of speech that makes declaration, 16b27, 21b21 and passim, for anything that is a declaration is also speech, even if speech does not include of itself the notion of assertion. All of this also shows why λόγος should never be translated 'speech,' for unlike φάσις, λόγος can never have significance while being without a structural relation between its limits, as clearly mere speech or φάσις can. These subtleties, when uniformly ignored in translations, help to make Aristotle and Plato difficult for one who does not know Greek, but are of inestimable aid in understanding when closely attended to.

At 2a34 the primacy of substance is seen in the fact that everything else that is 'stated' and therefore credited with 'existing,' is either 'stated by virtue of,' καθ᾽ ὑποκειμένων λέγεται, or 'exists in,' ἐν ὑποκειμέναις ἐστίν, primary substances, i.e. individual things. Individual things are therefore the basis of the resolution of the apparently amorphous flux of perception into 'limits' of being and discourse, i.e. whether regarded simply as the significances we talk about (definitions) or the things that exist (hypotheses).

With this we have the basic consideration that lies in back of Aristotle's 'categorizing' of entities stated in inquiry. Categorizing, as we also said in the closing chapter of our commentary on

Aristotle's *Nicomachean Ethics*, is one of the four essential factors in the determination of procedure in inquiry. Everything that exists is either an individual substance that exists by virtue of itself, or something derivative of it in its being. The proof of this, he says, is inductive. In Plato's logic, the 'limit' selected as the fundamental entity in statements, is the derivative 'form' or 'idea' which exists in a transcending hierarchy of being. For the sophists the comparable entity is a further derivative, the perspective of the speaker distinguishing himself from those opposing him and expressed as a 'type.'[11] For the atomists the 'limit' is the matter existing at varying levels of reduction and composition. Throughout history these four exhaust the derivative alternatives in the determination of what is categorized, or as McKeon says, selected, as the 'things' inquiry is about.

The procedure or mode of thought that Aristotle uses to determine the nature of the entities discussed in rational inquiry is called by McKeon resolution. For Aristotle's way is always to grasp 'things' by 'resolving' the interdependencies of varying factors that constitute any problem. Any predicate by which the specification of an entity is determined establishes that entity as a factor in an encompassing circumstance composed of such factors as needed to give the circumstance its function, unity and substance. For to resolve is to find a function within a circumstance for everything that is truly a part of that circumstance.

At 2b7 Aristotle starts a series of arguments showing the

11. When Walter Watson, in his book *The Architectonics of Meaning*, changed McKeon's term 'selection' to the 'perspective' of a text, he made several fatal mistakes. One is the assumption that his variables are those of any 'text,' for texts include poems, prayers, forensic debates, and even shear nonsense, but both Aristotle and McKeon talk only of the logic of inquiry. He has also confused it with the sophistic version of itself, as is patent from p.253 in the book of McKeon's essays, *Freedom and History and other Essays*. It is like calling all birds instances of sparrows. David Dilworth, in his book *Philosophy in World Perspective*, simply copies the errors without any critical examination.

dependence of all other existing things upon primary substance, as we have implied in our description of resolution. The other categories of existence are dependent in a different sense than forms and genera are. They are accidents of primary substances. For it only 'happens' that something is green, or moving, or five pounds heavy. Such categories do not touch the being of what 'is' in the primary sense. In the resolution of a substance, they are factored out of the solution. Secondary substances have the same relation to these other categories as primary substances do, which of course is the grounds for calling them substances at all.

We first ran into the verb 'to attribute' at 1a25. The root sense of ὑπάρχω which has been translated in countless ways, is 'to begin,' or 'to begin from under,' or 'to make a beginning,' and 'to spring up.' The verb implies that one thing finds its beginning or source of existence at a certain locus or in another thing. This may be a quality that thing has, its ability to effect something else, etc. Whenever one thing can be stated of another, as red is said of a rose, the first finds its 'beginning' in the second. What Aristotle calls τὰ ὑπάχοντα, 'attributes,' are therefore the 'things that have their beginning in the thing either 'of which,' or 'by virtue of which' they are stated or attributed, and thus 'attributes' means 'what belongs' to the thing, either accidently if 'of' is used, or essentially as 'by virtue of' indicates. The phrase at 2a16 ὁ τὶς ἄνθρωπος ἐν εἴδει μὲν ὑπάρχει τῷ ἀνθρώπῳ, therefore, is translated literally "a certain human in form is attributed 'to' [the form] human," not 'by virtue of' human [as a whole]. Because the atomic or indivisible substance is predicated 'by virtue of' nothing, only the form of the individual, and not the individual as such, is attributed to, and not by virtue of, the form of the species. But the individual's form is predicable of the species human only because it does not 'exist in' the individual. For whatever exists 'in' something exists nowhere else.

All of this is completely lost in the Oxford translation (E. M. Edghill) and the Loeb translation (H. P. Cooke) at 2a16. For not understanding the nature of Aristotle's conception of attribution, they turn Aristotle's statements into statistical and quantitative inclusions of individuals within species or classes within classes. But Aristotle is not talking of relations of classes on the model of Venn diagrams, Boolean logic, or Bertrand Russell's completely verbal form of logic, where any accidental factor makes a class of things. He is talking about stating certain things 'by virtue of' the nature of other things. Numerical inclusion does not touch this sense of predication or attribution. Such distortion occurs when a literal translation is eshewed for reasons irrelevant to the work, and one calls on one's own philosophic proclivities to do an interpretation, as above Watson did. There is a context in Aristotle's logic in which the terms of logic become merely numerical counters, namely in the *Prior Analytics*, but the concept is spurious here, and the translator should either be aware of what Aristotle's logic does, or simply and literally follow the Greek where it will.

From 2b7 the problem is to show that, to the degree a thing is removed from primary substance, its being is reduced. In Plato's view there is no difference in priority of being among the forms. But for Aristotle, not reality, but the basis of reality, starts with what exists by virtue of a whole, and there can be priorities between what is stated by virtue of a whole only if one assumes reality is first known in the perceptible nexus of all experience. For the sophists any category is equally capable of stating what is, for there is no 'is' save what a man 'measures' by his statements, and statements fix their own priorities. For the materialists like Democritus and Empedocles all priorities follow from the principle of reduction, and the simplest is most real.

For Aristotle all forms are themselves equally real, but forms, which belong among indivisible things, are more real than genera, which are simply the groupings of things by similarities. These two exhaust the secondary substances because none of the other categories of existence, how much, what sort, etc., make primary substance evident. This must be kept in mind in the attempt to understand Aristotle's treatment of any science, contemplative or practical. When one wishes to render 'what something is,' an atomic primary substance, one states appropriately form and genus. But in saying that it is so much, or of a certain sort, or is related to something in some way, one renders that substance 'in an alien way,' ἀλλοτρίως, 2b35. That is, by rendering the other categories one is not rendering the 'being' of anything, but its accidents, though this notion is not yet brought out.

At 2b37 the question turns from the differing properties of categorizations to the consequent relations between categories. The priorities are established. Primary substances are more commandingly stated substances because the other substances are stated by virtue of them. As primary substances are related to the other categories, so the secondary substances are related to the other categories. For all other categories are predicated by virtue of the secondary substances, by virtue of being predicated of the primary substances.

At 3a7 no substance, primary or secondary, exists in something, and of substances only the secondary are predicated by virtue of what underlies, and then only of primary substances. All the other categories exist things, and none are predicated by virtue of what underlies, though they may be simply predicated of what underlies. This difference fixes the limitation of scientific demonstration by determining the difference between the relation of secondary substances and the relation of the other categories to primary substance. For only what exists 'by virtue of' what underlies yields demonstration. Also, at 3a15, while the arguments[12] (including definitions) by virtue of secondary substances are predicated by virtue of primary substances, the arguments of the other categories are never even stated 'of' any substances, be-

12. The difference between 'definition,' ὁρισμός, and argument, λόγος, is crucial, yet translators continually confuse the two. Both can be principles, but one is a thesis and the other an hypothesis. Aristotle does not use his terms as carelessly as translators make him do.

cause they are only 'in' what underlies them and are not stated by virtue of it. The differences between the forms of a genus, 3a21, also do not exist in what underlies them, just as forms do not, but are predicated of them. So also the arguments of these differences are predicated of the things of which the differences are predicated, as whatever statements can be made about two-legged by virtue of a whole can be said of the thing that is two-legged, like knock-kneed.[13]

At 3a33 it is shown that the synonymous character of scientific demonstrations, or to put the matter in modern semantic terms, the univocal character of scientific language, is due to the fact that all predications of substances and differences are predicated synonymously. For substance and difference is predicated either by virtue of atomic things or by virtue of forms. Only when the predication is 'by virtue of' what underlies, and is not simply a predication 'of' what underlies, will the entities discussed by synonymous and the scientific terminology be univocal. The univocal characteristics of syllogistic reasoning, thus, are derived from the nature of predication. The things that are synonymous were defined back in Chapter 1, as the things of which both the name is common and the argument are the same. It will at the same time be evident why λόγος must not ever be translated 'definition,' ὁρισμός, for with univocal terms it is not simply the definition, but any proposition involving the entity that must hold.

Primary substance obviously is a categorization or category of nothing since it is predicated of nothing, while form is predicated of the atomic and genus is predicated of both the atomic and the form. The differences within the genus are also predicated of both atomic things and the forms of them. Also the argument, as something stated by virtue of both the form and the

13. This again shows that argument does not mean definition, for knock-kneed is not the definition of two-legged, yet is an argument stating a predication of it.

genus, is stated by virtue of the atomic thing, and the argument of the genus is stated by virtue of the form. The reason for this is that whatever is said by virtue of what underlies is also stated of whatever the underlying thing is stated. We thereby have another illustration that λόγος does not mean simply definition, and another illustration of the crucial importance of κατά. In precisely the same way the arguments of the differences are all stated of both the atomic things and the forms. Thus we have different things with the same name, of each of which the same argument is stated in every such case, which is the same as the definition of synonymous, 1a6.

Aristotle, therefore, expressed precisely the logical grounds upon which the justly famous *dictum de omne* rests, that it is the consequence, not the precondition, of all scientific predication. In the history of logic it was necessarily a sophistic or statistical approach to the syllogism that made this enormous change. It is not that you need it in order to have science, but that having science you will obtain it.

The consequence of the synonymous character of the topics of science, or in today's jargon the univocality of the terms of science, is the unity of substance, for all the predications of which we have been speaking make one thing evident, i.e. clarify one self-subsisting item of experience, a substance which is a 'this' of perception. We are mislead however by customary modes of speech that syntactically use forms and genus accidentally in the same way as substances. For signifying a 'sort' is not signifying a 'this.' And with this Aristotle has again confuted those linguists who have claimed that Aristotle's philosophy is derived from the nature of Greek syntax and grammatical structure. For here his departure from that 'norm' is evidence that Aristotle listens to another drummer.

Yet Aristotle must make a distinction even between 'sorts,' for while cats are a 'sort,' and green objects are a 'sort,' there is a world of difference between them, a difference to which Bertrand Russell's logic, and most logic texts, pay no attention. For

133

things specified by accidents are merely sorts, while sorts that are forms or genera signify the unities that subsist, i.e. are gounded in being, not happenstance. The other categories signify only what happen to be and therefore cannot possibly be things scientifically known, for they do not abide, and therefore are known only in the sense in which any accident is known.

At 3b24 Aristotle turns to the attributes of substance, and first that it has no contrary. But the lack of contraries is clearly not a property of substance, for quantities also have no contraries. Substance is not more or less substance, as other categories may be more or less, e.g. more or less white or beautiful. While not having a contrary, substance, being one and the same, accepts contraries, being at one moment this and at the next the contrary of this. For it is not the color that is at one moment white and the next black, but the substance to which the color is attributed. A survey of the categories (induction) shows that, unless it is thought that arguments can be false at one time and then true, the ability to accept contraries is attributed of no other existing thing, and therefore this is a property of substance. There must then be a digression to examine the charge that arguments and opinions also admit contraries.

The ability to change means that substances become alien to themselves. But what about arguments and opinions, do they accept the contraries of true and false? The argument "Someone is sitting,"[14] becomes now true, now false, not by itself changing, but by the thing being moved. Thus substance is the only category of being that admits contraries. It does this by itself no longer being the same in that respect. It is of course no part of this treatise, and therefore Aristotle does not mention it, but the accidental character of the attribution of the other categories,

14. That this should be called an argument is conclusive evidence that λόγος does not mean definition, but simply any predication grasped by reason. And since syllogism is based on predication, it is argument only because a predication is.

including the consequent possibility of contraries, and thus the loss of synonymous entities, is what limits science to the exploration of substance and difference.

This digression into the question of whether arguments also admit of contraries is also illustrative of the separation of the problems of the first two books of the *Organon*. For arguments are the structures of reason, the 'weaving together' of two or more entities understood, as the categories of this treatise. Obviously, the two problems become greatly confused if the topic of *Concerning Interpretation* has attributes essential and in common with the topic of the *Categories*. They would be systematically confused by any procedure not recognizing the need to make the analogous distinction. For there is no function in any procedure that does not have its analogue in the others.

We have now completed the examination of the first and most important of Aristotle's categorization of what is, substance. By this time it should be clear to a reader what this treatise called the *Categories* is doing. Its problem is to fix one factor, and one only, in man's attempt at inquiry, bringing significance, rationality, system and value to his experience of the world. The problem here is to determine what are the logical simples, the 'things,' the entities or items from which the complications or distinction in this way in inquiry. But any procedure will make a 'weavings together' of inquiry arise. The examination is then of the fundamental parts, the 'limits' of the analysis of inquiry. For inqiry is made of arguments, causally connected predications, which are based on prior arguments or predications discovered to reason, and these are analyzed into their constituent parts which are limits, simples, or the predicates and the things that underlie them. But as to whether these simples are limited to the categories of being, as the ancient title given to the treatise suggests, remains a problem still to be solved.

As from time to time we have attempted to indicate, in the history of thought, and even in such a short time span as classical Greece, this was done, well or badly, with or without a clear consciousness of what the inquirer was doing, in ways and modes of thought that are now clearly distinguishable. And the problem was adequately called by McKeon selection, for what the inquirer does, knowingly or not, is select, by the criterion of some cause, the 'things,' the limits in the analysis of arguments establishing what is, what is thought, or what is said. For experience does not come already with either its parts or its composites labeled and determined. And the sort of entities a man's procedure sees pertinent to discussion, has a good deal of latitude. By the manner in which inquiry is done these simples are selected or categorized by determining their structure through some cause. When projected against our statement of the variation of procedures, as in our commentary on Aristotle's *Nicomachean Ethics*, the procedure Aristotle uses to categorize the things of inquiry, is that of resolution, for entities are articulated by resolving their manifold relations to one another in terms of one that is primary.

Chapter 6. Of all the accidental categories, it is 'how much' that has the greatest part in scientific predication, and therefore the one to which Aristotle first turns. For there is a sense in which 'how much' can function as a topic of existential inquiry. Even the Greeks developed sciences that were substantive adjuncts to mathematics, namely harmonics, optics and what they called astrology. Modern science, by the domination since the Renaissance of the more reductive procedures of operational discrimination and materialistic structure, has arbitrarily limited its investigations to the measurable, or what is statable quantitatively. Most scientists today follow a statistical rather than a functional investigation of phenomena. The excuse is that what is measurable is both easier to handle and more exact. But Aristotle recognized, long before this tendency became institutionalized, the minimally scientific character of the applications of mathematics to existential matters, for he often refers to these adjuncts. But it was his insistence that true science is not so narrowly defined. For though a functional grasp of the contents of experience is not as precise, it enlarges greatly our grasp of what is.

As he did with substance, so with the category 'how much,' he first distinguishes kinds. The defined (limited, discrete) is distinguished from the continuous, and what involves placement from what does not. What is defined lacks common limits between entities, while the continuous does possess common boundaries. In this respect number is like argument[15] which is also from defined parts. The illustrations that come easiest to mind are of mathematical entities, numerical or geometric, but the continuous holds also of both place and time, where mathematics is applied to the phenomenal. At 4b32 there is an illustration of how the terms of logic can stand for thing, thought and word, for it is clear that it is as word (voice) that argument is 'how much' by having short and long syllables, and argument in this sense is built out of no common part, but the simplest parts are different in form.

Some things, like line, are continuous, for any limit is held in common by two parts, and this can be in one, two, or three dimensions. In the same way the time now is simply the limit joining what has gone by and what is still to come. Time is therefore defined by the motion of things. Place or space too, is defined by the occupation of body, and the limits of its joining are precisely those of the body joined.

The primary distinction, in the division of 'how much' into kinds, is that between what has 'placement,' θέσις, which is 'where' in space,[16] and what has order. For the parts of line have placement, but the parts of number have order. Those things that do not abide have no placement, such as moments in time. That which has no sequence has no order. Argument also has order but not placement.

All other things are 'how much' only by virtue of accident, as thinking might be called long because it happens to exist

15. Λόγος means here the same as at 4b9. It is φάσις, not λόγος, that means speech. Compare our comments p. 126.
16. And therefore should not be translated attitude or position.

through time. Aristotle is advising us to be careful of the things to which we attribute predicates, for accidental attribution has no force. For it is not 'by virtue of' what underlies that the attribution is made, as it is not by virtue of being white that so much magnitude is attributed to a surface. The color is not what 'commands' the attribution. We now see how vast are the ramifications of the mistranslation of κατά, for it governs all scientific attributions.

As indicated under substance, 'how much' also has no contrary, for nothing defined has a contrary. If, 5b14, many is held to be contrary to few, still these are relations, not quantities, and in fact what is many or few depends upon the context, adding to the relativity. But in fact, 5b30, many and few are not contraries, for what has contraries must be something grasped by virtue of itself, not by virtue of, or in relation to, something else. By this we see even greater extension to the influence of κατά. A contrary must be one of two attributes that exclude each other, yet because great and small are extrinsic denominations of a thing, it can be great and small simultaneously depending upon what external relation is implicated. The assumed contrariety in respect of 'how much' appears to stem mainly from matters of place, as above and below, and the extension to other matters is on the basis of analogy to this. But what is most proper to 'how much' is the question of equality, for this is attributed to no other category.

Chapter 7. The question of the order in which the categories are discussed should by now have arisen. For in many of the listings made by Aristotle the second category mentioned is quality. But now we see there are two categories are discussed prior to that one. The question should be asked, what is it about these categorizations of things isolated from experience that would affect the order of presentation? We have, from the discussion of the first two, already seen clues. It is clear that substance had to be discussed first because it is the basis of the being of the others. 'How much' is virtually a quasi-substance in the sense that it affords the topic of adjunctive sciences such as harmonics, optics and astrology, and today it virtually dominates scientific topics. And it is clear that relations are less substantial than quantities, for they are not attributions that hold of things by virtue of themselves as even the past chapter established. The first suggestion that pops to mind is clearly an order of priority determined by completeness of being. But why is relation discussed prior to quality? This may take a reading of both chapters.

Aristotle spends a long paragraph appealing to our intuitions concerning relations, for much hangs on accurate understanding of it. It has, as he shows, a far greater extension than common sense might grasp. The paragraph closes noting a possible confusion between two categories, being relative to something and being situated, κεῖσθαι, or laid.

A placement, θέσις, said to be an example of 'something related to something' at 6b6, is also the term he uses in the *Posterior Analytics* for the principles of demonstration, either definitions or hypotheses, which we have there translated thesis or assumption.[17] For the premisses of science about matters of fact need to be assumed by the student in learning the science in contrast to the axioms of demonstration of which the student must be convinced to learn anything. Such assumption or 'putting down,' is obviously relative to the 'place' at which it is put, as the principles are placed first before what is derived from them. Aristotle is afraid the reader will think that the seventh of his categories in Chapter 4 is reducible to the fourth of the categories listed there, (but the third considered here). That it is not is shown in the fact that 'to be lying down,' 'to be standing,' and 'to be sitting,' which are examples of the seventh category, 'being situated,' are not placements and therefore not relations to some-

17. This should be noted as one of the times in which the divergence of Greek and modern custom is so great as to necessitate two English words for one in Greek. For it seems unreasonably awkward to call the premisses of science 'placings' or 'placements,' though in fact that is just what they are.

thing, but they are derived from the placements that are relations. The difference is seen between the two words, the verb κάθηται, 'he sits,' used at 2a3 as an example of 'being situated, κεῖσθαι, and a noun from the same root, καθέδρα, 'a sitting,' used at 6b11 as a sort of placement which is a relation. To be sitting, καθῆσθαι, is not itself a placement, but a way of being situated, derived from the notion of sitting which is a relation to something. When we come to examine this seventh category in Chapter 9, 11b9, he will say what is stated here is sufficient.

When Aristotle listed the ten categories in Chapter 4, he listed relations after qualities, 1b29, but in discussing them he puts relations before qualities. The change may explain the καί in line 6b15 which indicates that in relations 'also' one finds contrariety, though neither substance nor 'how much' involve contraries, for qualities, as we will see in Chapter 8, do. This would seem to make the change in order quite deliberate.

Yet contrariety is not found in all relations. And while more and less are found in relations, this also is not true of all. More proper is the fact that in every relation there is reciprocation, or as Aristotle says, the relation 'turns around,' and if something is double of something, the other is half of what is double, so that either implies the other, and every relation exists as two and has two statements. Where it appears they do not 'turn around' it is because the relation has not been appropriately rendered, as wing is not the relative to bird, but winged thing is. This of course brings up the necessity of introducing words where customary language does not have the necessary precision, about which Aristotle spends a good deal of time. The reason, of course, is that sophist or operational reasoning, which recognizes only practical considerations, can only be thwarted by such precision. Even today, forensic and political haggles witness this truth.

The second point to be made, 7b15, is that the two terms in a relation must be simultaneous, ἅμα, which in spite of translations to the contrary, never means 'at the same time,' but always what is together in absolutely any relation of priority, whether

140

time, being, statistical numbering or whatever.[18] Relatives are also in most cases simultaneous in every sense of simultaneity because they are simultaneous in being, but there are exceptions. Most notable is the relation between science and what is knowable,[19] for the ability to be known must exist before the existence of the habit. The only sorts of science that exist simultaneously with its object are those in which reason in not regulative, but constitutive, as in the practical sciences. The proof of the priority of the knowable is that the removal of the science does not remove the object.[20] He first demonstrates this about objects of the understanding, 7b24, and then at 7b35 objects of perception. For the world does not cease to exist because no one perceives it. But of course it continues to exist without the perceiver only as perceptible, not as perceived.

An objection might be raised, 8a13, that while primary substances are not relative, secondary substances are. The problem concerns the organic parts of primary substances, the liver, heart, head, etc., which are substances in so far as they have functions and are existential units. If this is 'my' liver it would seem it exists in relation to me. Aristotle's answer, at 8a34, is that a thing is not itself relative to something simply by being stated 'of something else.' In order to state that the being of something is relative to something else, one must grasp that relation in order to make the statement. But what merely belongs to me, my golf club, my house, my liver, can be understood as golf club, house or liver without grasping its relation to me. But I can not be

18. A correctable item in Liddell and Scott, for first saying 'at once, at the same time,' to add 'mostly of time' is a careless correction. For it always means 'together,' 'simultaneous,' in any kind of priority.

19. Aristotle's statements about this relationship are vitiated by the translation of ἐπιστητόν as 'what is known.' The translation of this verbal adjective as what is, rather than what is able to be, is a violation of Greek grammar, as every lexicon shows.

20. Which of course shows that τὸ ἐπιστητόν is correctly translated as 'what is knowable,' not 'what is known.'

known as uncle without the simultaneous grasp of someone as nephew or niece to me. Both members of the relation must be grasped together in order even to claim the relation. But that 'my' golf club, 'my' house and 'my' liver are mine, is an extraneous matter to what is grasped. Nephew is therefore a relation, liver is not. For the substantial nature of the uncle is impossible without the inclusion of the nephew, but the substantial nature of my liver or my head does not include me.

Chapter 8. The categories of quantity and relation, though both dependent on substance, are both stated by virtue of themselves, with a mere notice that they are dependent. But quality is not even statable save in terms of the substance upon which its being depends. For their definition is "that by virtue of which we state of what sort people are." The dependence of the category upon substance for the first two is implicit in their definitions, nor is their any distinction between the kinds of substances on which they are dependent for their being. For quantity and relation are categories existing in, not predicated of, any substance whatever. But quality can be specified as existing in only certain substances, for a stone is not affected by all the qualities of another stone. An animal may be affected by man's justice, as rock affects rock, but is not perceptive of that justice. Therefore, the full range of the category of quality must specify the substance to which it is attributed as man, not merely animate or natural being. The reason, we will find, is that the 'sorts' that are exhibited by things are a function of the level of being of that which perceives it. Thus not only do certain qualities exist in only certain substances, but qualities exists only for certain levels of being. This obviously is a reduced level of being, and accounts for the change in the order in which he lists the categories, and indicates that it is indeed being that orders them.

A second point is that this is the first of the accidental categories to be given what is linguistically the form of a noun, by adding to the adjective the inflection for the noun, giving ποιότης, a quality or 'a sort.' Plato, in the *Theaetetus*, 182A, apologizes for his use of this word as being ἀλλόκοτό ὄνομα, 'an alien name.' It is one of the terms lately arising from the growing needs of greater philosophic precision in Greece's recent intellectual rise, which is far beyond the limited capacity of its neighbors. Aristotle uses the comparable noun ποσότης in the *Metaphysics*, but nowhere in the *Categories*. It seems clear that he uses this noun as long as Plato has set the example, but even in his private archives, he does not show the modern sophomoric delight in verbal innovation, but responds to necessity only.

Habit, ἕξις, and disposition, διάθεσις, are one 'form' of quality, and differ in that the first is 'more able to abide' and 'exists for more time.' Aristotle states only a difference in degree, not in form, and in fact recognizes the inadequacy of this at 9a4-13. The question of duration, of course, points to the accidental quality of these in respect of substance. The next form of quality, at 9a14, are the natural powers which are yet not part of the nature of the substance, else they would not be one of a pair of contraries predicable of the substance. They are therefore natural only to individual natures, not to forms. No doubt Aristotle lists these second to take advantage of the analogy of their being to habits and dispositions, since they are not the 'substantive sorts' found in forms and genera.

The third form of quality, at 9a28, best shows the dependence upon substance, for the argument in essence is that the presence in the percipient substance of a quality is the evidence of the corresponding productive quality in the object perceived. Aristotle is concerned that it be properly determined what is active and what is passive in this matter. The term παθητικός, 'pathetic,' not in our twisted sense, but meaning 'able to affect,' 'affective,' as even in English the inflection originally meant, in contrast to the term παθητός, 'affectable,' does not mean the object is affected, or itself undergoes the attribute, as implied by our twisted notion, but it means, as do all terms with the inflection ικός, as well as the English inflection '-ive,' that the object produces the attribute in something else, the percipient being.

This is why qualities generally were defined in terms of the percipient substance rather than simply in terms of the object to which they are imputed. That such matters are more accurately expressed in Greek than in English is seen in the passive construction of the Greek verb αἰσθάνομαι compared with the misleading active construction of the English word 'to perceive,' which suggests that the form is an initiation of the perceiver, as in fact some early Greek thinkers held, rather than something received from the object. For even if modern science wishes to credit the resulting form to the potentialities of the percipient, Aristotle wishes to point out that the imputation of its source of being lies in the perceived object. In other words, whatever the differences of form, just as the motions of the object moved may be different than the motion of the moving object, the being of the quality, as the being of the motion, lies in the agent, not the patient, and the agent is the colored object, not the patient that perceives the color.

Again, he distinguishes between those of an enduring nature which are called affective qualities, as the tendency to dark complexion, and those that are transient and called simply passions, πάθη. And a passion is simply what befalls us, not the sort we are. There is also a distinction between the passion as a faculty of the percipient, πάθη, and passion as the objectification of that faculty, πάθημα, but few translators pay much attention to the difference. When that affection or passion becomes steadfast, it is then called a quality in the full sense, 9b19. These are the things by virtue of which we are stated to be of a 'sort,' while they remain mere passions or affections if they are not steadfast. Some of these are qualities and passions of the soul, rather than the body, 9b33, for they are the 'sorts' of our functions or activities.

A fourth kind of quality, 10a11, are the figure, σχῆμα, and shape, μορφή, which exist in substance. Figure or schema and shape are attributed in respect of the wholeness of a thing, for being triangular, or square, or curved the thing is stated of some

144

sort. But some things which to common parlance might be thought as qualities he says are not, for things like rare and dense or rough and smooth are due more likely to the placement of parts in respect of one another, than to any form attributable of the whole,[21] and insofar as they exist because of the parts, they do not have the being of quality. It is clear by this that the categories of being, though a priori to any particular investigation, are a posteriori to experience generally, induced from fact.

It is clear at this point that Aristotle's statements about qualities and their sorts has progressed, as does the order of the categories, in terms of the being of the topic, though here the order is from less to more, while the categories are listed from more to less.

At 10a27 Aristotle turns to other predicates that are qualities as derivative from other things. The derivative nature of these is obvious if that from which the quality is derived has been given a name. For example, what is grammatical is derivatively named quality as derived from the art of grammar. But if we lack a word for the primary or original entity, the derivative nature is often obscure. Thus one who is naturally able to run, δρομικός,[22] is so named derivatively by virtue of a natural power than is not named, and therefore the derivative nature of the quality is not obvious.

Sometimes, 10b5, the language is so constructed that even though the thing from which the quality is derived is named the derivation is not obvious because the names do not indicate the derivation, as 'worthy,' σπουδαῖος, by its verbal disimilarity is not seen to be drived from 'virtue,' ἀρετή.[23]

21. Since the distance or interval between parts is not an attribute of the whole, such things are attributable in respect of the matter.
22. Here again the Greeks had an inflectional word while we do not. It would be perhaps 'runative,' on the model of others.
23. This shows derivatives are things, not words, one thing being derived from another thing, and words only as a consequence, for verbally there is no derivation of σπουδαῖος from ἀρετή.

In the case of some qualities, by virtue of what they are, contrariety is attributed to them, as the quality justice is the contrary of injustice. But not all qualities, for there is no contrary to yellow or any color. Also, if one part of a contrary is a quality, so is the other. Qualities also admit of degrees, even of the same thing at different times, though this is disputed, for some say, 10b32, that the things that possess the quality may possess it more or less, but the quality itself is not more or less.[24] But some qualities, as geometric shapes, do not seem to admit of degrees, for the argument stating what these shapes are, applies or not. It is clear that one disputing this could do so only on the basis of practical utilities, not science.

None of these matters, however, are proper to quality, since they all involve exceptions. But similarity and dissimilarity is proper to quality, and it is only by virtue of being a 'sort' that two things are stated similar or dissimilar. His closing comments on quality are a defense of the notion that a thing may be categorized in more than one form of being. For qualities such as habits and dispositions are relative to somethings, those at least that are genera, if not the particular forms. There is a science of grammar, but grammar itself is not grammatical of anything.

24. This is the second time in two pages, the first is at 10a29, that a quality, ποιότης, is distinguished from the thing that has the quality, τὸ ποιόν. Yet Edghill flatly denies it, and both he and Cooke translate the two by the same term. Aristotle is distinguishing between the form of a thing and the thing possessing the form, a sunolon of form and matter. Even Liddell and Scott are confused in saying outright that "τὸ ποιόν = ποιότης." Cf. p 1238, 8th edition, or p 1431 of the 1948 reprint. They cite 1083a11 as authority, but all that says is that 'what is one' is the monad, not that it is the same as unity. For the monad is not unity either, but the existing thing used as a measuring unit. Incidentally, Liddell and Scott also err in giving 'the black,' τό μέλαν as 'black pigment,' and in their small dictionaries, 'blackness,' μελανία, as 'a black cloud,' though they avoid such a sophomoric mistake in the big lexicon. There are in fact many cases of Liddell and Scott erroneously giving a species for a term that stands for a genus.

Chapter 9. There are still six of the ten categories remaining to be discussed, but these, Aristotle indicates, present no great problems in the determination of their meaning, their properties, or the place they play in inquiry, and therefore he treats them rather summarily. Producing and suffering admit both of contraries and more and less. What was stated of something 'being situated,' τὸ κεῖσθαι or how something 'lies,' or is oriented or arranged, back at 6b13 when 'things relative to something' was being discussed, that this mode of being is derivative of the relation of placement, θέσις, he says is sufficient for the purposes of determining the place or locus in inquiry of such a mode. It is clear that Aristotle regards 'being situated' as a way of being without stating a relation to another thing, but not as being independent, as being substance is, because it is derived from a relation to something else, since θέσις, 'placement' or 'being put or placed' indicates the origin of the denomination, while the new category simply omits this reference. So also he dismisses when, where, and possessing, for what they are he says is apparent.

But editors have been unhappy both about this chapter and the ones following, and have tried to devise other explanations for what they read. The issue is of such importance that we must break into our commentary to dealt with it adequately. Lines 11b1-7 which discuss only producing and suffering, it is argued by Minio-Paluello, should be moved to follow line 11a14, where they then interrupt the flow of the discussion about qualities. The thing that is so irksome about this, is that Minio-Paluello has so little regard of his reader that he does not even give his reasons for such a drastic change. Like a parent who cares nothing for the child's development of his faculties for life, but says to him "Do as I say," or like a church that cares nothing for the moral character of its parishioners but only for what they do, and says, "It is god's will." It is an example of the teacher who thinks knowing is saying the right words, or the moralist who thinks morality is doing what the law prescribes. But a little thought and we can see what Minio-Paluello is about. And it is worth our trouble to see what this is.

From 10b26 to 11a14 Aristotle discusses the fact that qualities, like many other things, admit or more and less. But this is by no means the place at which 'more and less' is discussed as a topic, for at 3b33 he discussed more and less as it related to substance, at 6a19 he discussed it as it related to how much, and at 6b21 as it related to what is relative to something. What then is the logic of saying that the discussion of more and less as it relates to the category of 'being situated' belongs with its discussion under the category of quality? This happens when one does not attend the author's own statements of his procedures.

Then the lines 11b8-14 are treated by Minio-Paluello as having so little worth that they are put in small type and bracketed so as to lose Bekker's lineage, as though they are unworthy of the reader's attention, and marked to be expunged. The footnote does not state why, as one would expect it to, but refers the reader to a paragraph in his Preface. There, on p.v, Minio-Paluello tells us that "Some have said the *Categories* are an 'imperfect' and not 'politum,' [i.e. not polite in the sense of polished] book written by Aristotle, but with no probable reason, since the whole is prefaced with Aristotle being the author, if one excepts seven lines 11b1-16 and certain words here and there. It is not certain that the parts are of a single work which is inscribed under the name *Categories*, but the final chapters, 11b17 - 15b32, which they furthermore called Postpraedicamenta, Andronicus suspected, not ineptly, to have been appended here from another place." He goes on to record other doubts by scholars, including some about *Concerning Interpretation*, but concludes that "Henricus Maier has shown correctly as it seems to us, that there is nothing that is not Aristotelian."

Thus he gives us his *imprimatur* in respect of the whole, but casually expunges things 'here and there.' What is to be noted of this speaking 'ex cathedra,' is the arrogation the speaker makes to himself of such authority as needs the citation of no evidence, a sort of grand sophistry that says 'my saying it makes it so.' For he gives no reason for any claim that the whole is Aristotle's, nor any reason why any parts cited should not also be so regarded. This is the arrogance of W. D. Ross, in assuming the translator owes the reader no explanation for the changes he makes, taken to new heights, for it is now expressly stated as a principle of scholarship. In the very same year, 1949, Harold Cooke, when he came out with his edition and translation for Loeb, announced, in a footnote at the end of Chapter 9, that the following chapters 'are commonly regarded by scholars as spurious.' But of course the last six chapters that discuss the 'post-predicaments,' are spurious only because the 'post-predicaments' are not categories, and it was already erroneously decided long ago by someone like Andronicus of Rhodes that the treatise is about categories. This is the scholars' version of the dictum not to disturb people with the facts when their minds are already made up without them.

Chapter 10. It is this chapter, and the topics it discusses, that shows, that the ancient editor who gave this treatise its title badly misconstrued what it is about. Some modern commentators have added ridiculously to the confusion by claiming, on the basis of the erroneous title, that this section of the treatise must be spurious. But if we keep in mind what logic is about, and contrast this treatise with the rest, the air may be cleared. The things discussed by Aristotle in *Concerning Interpretation* he says are all syntheses. For truth and falsity are the properties of reason's connection or disconnection of entities first grasped by understanding. For it is only by making predications, one entity attributed to another, that one effects either a correspondence or a lack of correspondence to what exists, for understanding cannot be false, since defining determines nothing that exists.

The topic of the *Categories*, then, is not categories or predicatings, but the definable limits, ὅροι, of which arguments are made, that are not functionally further divided. The 'categories of being' are only the more obvious limits that statements employ in making syntheses. The least thought reveals that there must be others, as relations between them. The word 'postpredicament' is a simplistic and ostensive, rather than functional, way of referring to these other limits. But the problem is, few scholars observed that these post-predicaments are just as simple in nature as the categories are. An 'opposite' is a significance, beyond the categories of being, which is not synthesized or put together, συντίθημι, or sometimes 'woven together' or complicated, συμπλέκω.

These are not 'woven together' by reason, but grasped by the understanding, for stating opposition affirms no more about what exists than stating substance or quality. The word 'proposed,' in the first sentence of Chapter 10 shows the number of these simples are a matter of experiential fact and no claim is made of their being exhaustive.

The categories are manners of existing intrinsic to the thing. We now turn to simple ways of existing in relation to another. He starts by distinguishing the ways in which we are accustomed to 'placing against' one another, ἀντιτίθεσθαι, or 'antitheticating,' things opposed, τῶν ἀντικειμένων. For an opposition, just as a category, is a simple existence or limit. There are four ways in which simples may be opposed, as things that are related, τὰ πρός τι, as contraries, ἐναντία,[25] as privation, στέρησις, and habit,[26] ἕξις, and as affirming and negating. Thus, while being a relative is an intrinsic property and a category, the relation of

25. Contraries are thus only one form of opposition, and the two should always be distinguished. When translators confuse them, as most do, it is like putting monkeys for primates or primates for monkeys.

26. Most scholars are exceedingly wary of translating ἕξις literally, as habit, to show its origin from ἔχω, habeo, to have, especially in the *Nicomachean Ethics* where its correct translation is crucial. This wariness is probably because of the mechanical interpretation of habit in behavioral psychology. Edghill and Cooke both translate it 'positive' as though 'having and privation' were a matter of turning something on or off. Such a translation turns a functional relation into a statistical one of mere presence or absence, but it is clear this is not Aristotle's meaning, for to 'have' a way of doing is not merely that it is attributed, but that it is closely bound up with what one is, just as the habit one wears.

150

opposition or contrariety is other than the things so related, for we talk of the relation without talking of the things related.

In the case of things opposed as relatives, either one in a relation is stated in reference to the other member of the opposition. But when the opposition is between contraries, the statement of one is not made in reference to the other member of the pair. An uncle is the uncle of his nephew, but the good is not the good of the bad. Some contraries have a middle, some do not, and in the latter, if one is not attributed, the other is. Odd and even exemplify the first, black and white exemplify contraries that have a middle alternative, like green.

Privation and habit, he says, are stated of the same thing, though they are not relations, for sight is not the sight of blindness as uncle is the uncle of nephew. The main problem concerning habit and privation is confusion between privation, when an attribute natural to something is missing, and the thing is indeed deprived of what is natural to it, and a lack which is natural to the thing so that not having the attribute is no privation to the thing's nature.

The characteristics of privation and habit differ also from contraries. Contraries, we remember, either do or do not have a middle. In the case of those that do not, as sighted and blind, it is not always necessary, as with contraries, that one or the other be attributed, for an animal not yet sighted is not blind. Of contraries that have a middle, as hot and cold have warm or tepid, if only one contrary is by nature attributed, as fire is hot and snow is cold, it is not necessary that the other be attributed to what receives it, the fire or snow. But in the case of privation and habit this necessity is indeed present, and what is receptive of the faculty, when it is receptive, is either sighted or blind. The opposition, then, between privation and habit, 13a15, is like neither sort of contrary. Also, unless one of a pair of contraries is attributed by nature, as fire is always hot, the thing is receptive of both contraries. But such change is impossible in the case of privation and habit, for change from privation to habit is impossible, as from being blind it is impossible to become seeing.

The opposition between affirming and negating is like none of the others, for they alone are true or false. The only things that are possible of being true or false are things that have been woven or put together by man's reason, 13b10, and all the other oppositions are simples, things grasped by man's understanding as entities, not predications as are both affirming and negating.

What would seem the most to be true or false, 13b12, are contraries that arise from reason putting entities together, as two statements that something is either of two contraries, as Socrates is healthy is the contrary of Socrates is sick. But of these it is not always necessary that one is true and the other false, for only if Socrates exists is this so. If he does not exist they are both false. Of privation and habit also, if the thing does not exist neither is true. But even if it exists it is not always true that one or the other is true. But in the case of affirming and negating, whether the thing exists or not, one is true and the other false. And this is the relation of contradiction, not that of contrariety.

Chapter 11. The problem turns to any possible implications for existence among contraries, as opposed to implications of meaning. The contrary to an entity may be more than one, as for example when it is a mean, for it will be contrary to both extremes. These in turn will be contrary not only to the mean but also to each other, but mostly to the mean. It is also not necessary that both contraries exist if one does, and sometimes it will not be possible.

Chapter 12. The topic of priority gives four meanings. Priority in respect of time is primary as well as most commanding. The second priority is 'what does not turn about by virtue of its sequence of being,' as while 1 is prior to 2, still 2 is not prior to 1. What is noteworthy is his statement that this is a priority of existence, for numbers exist as the abstractable forms of existents, and therefore exist as well as the things from which they are abstracted, but in the way that numbers exist, not as the things do. This shows the phenomenal basis even of abstractions.

For with a person who regards mathematics as an ideational conception having no necessary relation to experience, but applied by right of its practical fruits, it would not be true that 'while the existence of 2 implies the existence of 1, the existence of 1 says nothing about the existence of 2.' For in a procedure of thought in which 1 is a number, it has no priority over other members of the sequence, but functions exactly as they, as the arbitrary application of an ideal system to existents. In such a statistical scheme 1 has no other basis than 2, and the entire system to infinity comes about by the same postulation. In Aristotle's procedure, it is only because the basis for number is phenomena, with numbers being the count of a selected existential unit, that 2 is dependent for its being upon 1. For it is only of existing things that the counting of two presupposes the prior existence of the measuring unit. Thus the priority of the measuring unit is a function of his phenomenal interpretation, and this interpretation involves the existence of number. The second priority is then the priority of existence, as the parents are prior, not only in time, but in being.

The third priority is that of order, which is the priority a statistical procedure would give to numbers, rather than the priority in being given by Aristotle. In an analytical study, such as mathematics, since there can be no priority of being, for the being of the triangle does not depend upon the being of the sides or angles, but all exist equally as potentialities of what is, there is still a priority in respect of the dependency of the intelligibility of the constructs upon the parts from which they are constructed. The same thing is true of language and its parts. In arguments also the relation of introduction to the narration is not like the relation of principle to demonstrated conclusion, which is indeed a priority of being. Priority of the better or more honored is also a priority simply of order and not of being. By better it is clear that Aristotle does not mean better in a functional sense, as that a constitutional state is better than a democracy, for better in the sense of more complete would be a priority of being. Here he means better in the sense of one's 'betters,' the way in which social classes are agreed upon. That the respect in which the many make those more honored and more cherished is 'the most alien' manner of using priority of order, is incredibly revealing of the man's most intimate perception of justice. For not only does he deny by this that a ruler is better in being than the ruled, but in an alien way even in respect of order.

There is a fourth sense of priority that involves things whose being turn about, that is, have no priority in that respect. In such a case, if one is the cause of the other, even though they are simultaneous in being, that one is prior. Thus the existence of human and the argument stating that he exists are simultaneous in being, for if one is true then the other is also. But there is no way that the truth of the argument about human could cause the existence of human,[27] while 'in a way' the thing is the cause of the truth of the argument. One notices, then, that for Aristotle what exists is a 'cause' of the truth of statements only by virtue of a metaphor.

Chapter 13. The question of priority brings up the question of simultaneity, which is not the same as existing at the same time, though some dictionaries, written under the aegis of reductive procedures, suggest it. Yet that their genesis be at the same time is the simple and most commanding meaning, according to Aristotle, of two things being simultaneous. Things are also simultaneous by nature which turn about by virtue of their sequence of being, as in relations where neither is the cause of the other. So also the differentiae of the same genus are simultaneous, for it is the same division of the same kind that partitions them. In the relation between genus and species or forms, however, the genera are prior and not simultaneous, for differences presuppose the being of the kind, but the kind does not presuppose the existence of the differences.

27. There is an argument for the existence of god that is claimed to violate this dictum.

154

Chapter 14. Other simples that need to be defined before being presupposed by reason's act of forming predications, are the six forms of motion. Aristotle assumes that it is obvious these six are distinct from each other. The only question is whether or not alteration can be reduced to one of the others. Presumably Aristotle is responding to the materialist's claim that alteration is simply the result of material increase or decrease through change of place. But Aristotle shows that if it were the same as any other, such as increase or decrease, every case of alteration would be a case of increase or decrease, and every case of increase or decrease would issue in an alteration. But this is obviously not so.

The contrary of motion without qualification of the kind of motion, i.e. simply, is rest. But in respect of the different forms of motion there are specific contraries. There might be some problem of articulating the contrary of alteration.

Chapter 15. The last simple to be discussed is 'possessing.' The word he uses is the infinitive of the verb 'to have' or 'to hold,' within a phrase formed by the article, as we would say 'the having,' or 'the holding.' The question naturally rises as to the difference between this and the eighth category, 2a3 and 11b11, which was expressed by the same verb, ἔχειν, but without the article, τὸ ἔχειν, as the other categories were also expressed. The article, of course simply is a verbal pointer, and it does not seem there is any difference between listing 'having' and 'the having.'

'Having' he says is stated 'in many manners,' and he goes through a list of them, inducing the general meaning through an appeal to one's immediate grasp of their commonality. Here at 15b28, as in the case of priority, at 14b7, he cites a 'most alien' use of the term in respect of a social relation. But where before he calls the political relation of civil inferiority an alien sense of priority, here he cites the 'having' of a woman an alien sense of possession.

The only difference between the entry for 'having,' ἔχειν, here and in the discussion of the categories, would seem to be that evidenced by the two parts of the treatise, to which we should in any case turn.

The ten categories are, if you will, the most general kinds of 'accusings' by which the soul formulates entities from the flow of experience when it attempts to make any sort of statement. These are then a presumed exhaustive list of manners in which the flow of experience is suitably and functionally divided into existents needed to produce the higher, more complicated forms of speech, such as arguments, syllogisms, etc., all involved in the attempt to discover and 'state' the rationality of experience. But the 'things' discussed from Chapter 10 on, are not so much the entities into which experience is dividable, as those simplicities exhibited by entities prior to and independent of any predication by man's reason that would implicate existence and therefore truth and falsity. They were, in the order discussed, in Chapter 10, oppositions, of which there were four sorts, things relative to something, contraries, privation and habit, and affirming and negating, in Chapter 11, implications of existence as properties of contraries, in Chapter 12, relations of priority, also of four sorts, in Chapter 13, relations of simultaneity, in Chapter 14, the sorts of motion of which entities are capable, and finally in Chapter 15, the relation between things through possessing.

Two important truths should now be obvious concerning the topic discussed in the *Categories*. One is that only the most naïve of philosophical stances could hold, as the logical positivists did, that the 'things' about which science makes it attributions are not themselves the products of thought, and take reason to articulate. The very fact that Aristotle criticizes the attempts of others to formulate the nature of the 'things' to which it addresses its inquiry, that there are problems as to how the task is properly or adequately accomplished, shows that the task is a legitimate part of the investigation of the procedure of science. The cries of Moritz Schlick, A. J. Ayer, and others with reductive tendencies, are thus simlistic errors, that all we need are facts, the notion that not only are the 'things' or 'entities' of experience simply given, but the propositions also in which they appear, and that neither the things (categories) nor the propositions (interpretations) need any intellectual effort to discern.

But the second truth that should now be clear, is that the 'things' which are the topics of science and the product of such inquiry, are derivative in nature, depending completely, (since they are the product of thought and reason), upon the mode of thought or the procedure used in their determination. For all thinking and reasoning is the instrumental use of one or more of the causes explaining what is. And cause, being a derivative thing, establishing answers more or less substantively, gives us a range of answers to our questions that vary, by the cause we choose, from the incomplete to the complete. Thus the selections, identified by McKeon as arising from differing modes of thought, vary in their adequacy to the full range of experience, from the most incomplete, the matters identified by the material cause used in structure, to the types of perspective identified by the initiating cause used in descrimination, to the transcending hierarchies of forms identified by the formal cause used in assimilation, finally to the most complete, the functional kinds identified by the completing cause used in resolution. What Aristotle has succeeded in showing in this treatise, is that, in this problem of determining the 'accusings' found in the statements of science, his procedure is able to include all that is accomplished in the others by their less inclusive causes, and in addition to indicate the completeness of being on which all the others in fact depend.

What a 'thing' or topic of speech is, therefore, for Aristotle, is a matter of the way in which it exists, ranging from the independent existence of a substance to the various dependent existences of the accidents of substance. But there is no difference between an examination of the causes of a thing's existence and the determination of the way in which it exists. In comparison with this manner of 'stating' things as referents for speech and thought, the 'things' produced by the other three procedures, by structure, discrimination, and assimilation, are of derivative completion, for the fact that they define the thing in terms of different and less complete causes than that by which resolution does the job. For at the minimum, for the atomists using structure, a thing is a matter that may be divided or compounded. For the sophists using discrimination, it is the type fixed by the perspective of a speaker. For a dialectician like Plato using assimilation it is a hierarchy of static forms. It is clear, then, that even though the determination of categories of existence, thought, or language, does not involve the formation of predications, for definitions do not implicate existence, yet categories are the result of procedures of thought, since they are 'the things of which phenomena are stated to consist.' And since all statements in which the predicate exists by virtue of 'what underlies,' what underlies must take the form of a cause of what is predicated, else the predicate could not exist by virtue of what underlies, it is only as a effect of what underlies that is it possible for them to exist. These categorizings, therefore, are seen to be derivative by making use of cause in derivative forms, respectively of the material, initiating, and formal causes, because the procedure has been respectively structure, discrimination, and assimilation, all of which lend incompleteness to the process. Aristotle's manner of categorizing, resolution, is the most encompassing, since it is based on cause in the sense of completion, which necessarily includes all the others as contributing to that completion.

The causes, then, and the fact they entail by their own nature the distinction between forms of reason that vary in completeness by the cause that is employed, are of the greatest importance in the understanding of any intellectual task. Whatever task to which we address ourselves, the understanding of what we are doing is enhanced the most by the correct grasp of what sort of cause is it on the basis of which our claims are made. For the identification of that cause is the clue to the adequacy of our claim.

COMMENTARY ON

CONCERNING INTERPRETATION

The names of Aristotle's treatises, given by others, reveal the view held of their contents by those ancient editors. Sometimes these editors understood these treatises, sometimes they were confused. *Categories* is derived from agora, ἀγορά, the public meeting place, or market, in each community, the 'assembly,' or 'the public togetherness,' from the verb meaning to gather or assemble, ἀγείρω. From this sprang a host of associated words, as οἱ ἀγοραῖοι, those frequenting public places, as hucksters, idlers, and even gods making public appearances. The verb ἀγορεύω meant to go public, or to speak publicly, the verb κατηγορέω, speaking down upon, κατά, and so to accuse. Thus, to categorize is to make a public predication, one thing of another. *Categories* are thus not a list of words, but accusations or predicatings of the flow of experience, a discrimination of things found in phenomena, greatly varying in substantiality or independence of existence. Yet the treatise we saw is about more than categories, including also the simple relations between.

'Things,' therefore, by Aristotle's complete procedure, are not simply (1) the matter of things, as the atomists and the Anatolians thought, nor (2) merely the subjective view of things, as the sophists held, nor (3) a hierarchy of hypostatized and encompassing forms, as the Platonists argued, but all of these secondarily, while primarily things are (4) substances having independent existence on which all the others depend, the matters, types, and hierarchy of forms, claimed by the other procedures. The categories, then, are the ways things are conceived to exist, through what is supposed to be the cause of existence. A catego-

159

ry is not a predication, and therefore its statement does not imply anything existing, but is that of which predications are made. Each of the four functions of 'stating,' including categorizing, depends on a sense in which there is existence, for 'to state,' λέγω, is precisely to assert existence. Categories, therefore, are existences only by the use of a cause, the 'why' of existence, just as the other functions of inquiry, interpretation, method, and principle. For categories are 'the things of which phenomena are stated to consist,' and that things 'are' or exist in all these senses, and not in one only, is the great point of Aristotle's *Categories*. In all statements in which the predicate exists by virtue of 'what underlies,' the predicate is caused by what underlies. If it were not, there would be no demonstration. The other three categorizations are thus derivative by making use of a derivative cause, respectively the material, initiating, and formal causes. Aristotle's manner of categorizing is the most encompassing, because only the completion of potentialities, by nature, includes all other things contributing to what is.

The title of this treatise, *Concerning Interpretation*, Περί Ἑρμηνείας, or 'Concerning Hermeneutics,' means 'of things that occupied Hermes.' Hermes was the messenger of the gods and the son of Zeus and Maia, daughter of Atlas. He carried messages in both directions, for he was not only herald to the gods, but the psychopomp of the dead on their way to Hades. He was also the master of scheming, or the manipulator of seemings. If then, we allow ancient myth to speak its mind, as Aristotle to his credit certainly does, for a myth is a way of stating in metaphor what is felt to be literally inexpressible, yet no less significant, the term ἑρμήνευμα is establishing the relation between the eternally divine and the ephemerally mortal, incorporating the function of both the psychopomp and the messenger. In the rules of interpretation are contained the means by which what is stated can have a referent that exists, either by being the material of what is,

1. Not simply a material part, but a logical part, such as a cause.

the source of what is, the structure of what is, or the completion of what is. For statements or predications relate to reality through the same latitude of causes that establish the categories talked about. In other words, the basis of the relation of human expression to reality, also, is some derivative of cause, just as in our next volumes we will find it is some derivative of cause that is either (3) the basis of the connections between propositions in the formation of method, or (4) the the basis of the self-evidence that makes what is given a principle. And it is this involvement of cause in logical functions that is missing in McKeon's account.

Interpretation, then, establishes the connection between expression and existence in statement or predication, and the variation of this connection in the derivative procedures of inquiry is the result of which cause is used to determine existence or being, since cause is derivative, accounting for existence more or less completely. When reality is formulated by virtue of either (1) the materials out of which the dynamism of phenomenal experience arises, or (2) the structures that inform such experience, it can only be a static reality, either underlying or transcending phenomenal events, not the moving thing itself that is perceived, but rather something assumed to be the static basis of what is dynamic. But when reality is formulated by virtue of either (3) the initiations of motions, or (4) the completions of motions, then what is real belongs to the moving phenomena of experience itself. Thus, McKeon, recounting the facts of inquiry rather than its causes, stated that the first distinction is whether reality is what is experienced or what lies behind experience, while we suppose that this distinction is procedurally a consequence of the choice of cause. For matter and form are by their nature static, while initiation and completion are by nature aspects of motion. This in itself is a sign that approaching procedure through the causes is more basic than the factual matters used by McKeon which allowed him to formulate procedures as arbitrary points of view or modes of thought, rather than as derivatives of a single and complete procedure.

161

As long as one is simply categorizing sorts of things predicated in any 'stating,' as in the *Categories*, there is, as Aristotle says, no necessary implication of reality or that to which the words refer. Thus, as stated in the *Posterior Analytics*, principles or unproved premisses are either theses or hypotheses. Only the establishment of predications between things stated, hypotheses, implicates a relation with reality. This relation lies in the connection between 'names,' ὀνόματα, things assumed to be 'known'[2] or grasped, and 'expressions,'[3] ῥήματα, the attributes expressed of things named, and only in this asserted connection is there implicated a relationship between what we are stating and what is. These two, names and expressions are discussed in chapter 2. They are not nouns and verbs in our modern sense, which are the functional parts of sentences constructed to many purposes other than inquiry. Names and expressions are instead the functional and existent parts of arguments, logical structures, asserted to exist in the effort to state what is.

But that is all that is implicated at this level of the analysis of inquiry, just that the form of predication is able to implicate reality, but whether this has been done or not, takes other steps still to come, syllogism, the linking of predications, and principle. Whether the relationship between words and reality has been established or not, is a question of the grounds or causes that mediate between expression and name, and constitutes the next stage of logic, taken up in the *Prior Analytics*. All that is now being discussed, is the required nature of predication, expressions stated of names, in such a way as to make possible a relation between that 'stating' and what is, a relation which we call the truth of the statements made.

2. As Liddell and Scott say, ὄνομα comes from the same root, γνο, as both the verb γιγνώσκω, 'to know,' and the noun νοῦς, 'understanding.'

3. It is equally significant that the word ῥῆμα, 'expression,' comes from the verb ἐρῶ which as we said is from the verb 'to flow,' ῥέω, and not from λέγω which concerns the articulated.

For even the things we categorize or accuse, are established as real only through propositions, statements, claims, by argumentation that attaches expressions to things named. In the case of principles the connection of these statements is a dialectic. In the case of properties, grounded upon principles stating the nature of things, the connection is a demonstration. This is why Aristotle says that defining states nothing about reality, and why the term 'argument,' λόγος, never means 'definition,' ὁρισμός, though every translator of the *Organon* has made this incredible assumption. Truth and falsity become possible only when the mind forms a complex, something attributed to something else, even if what is attributed is only bare existence. For the uncomplicated, simple thing by itself cannot be false.

In stating the rules by which expressions are attributed to things named, by the implication of one of the four causes, we reveal the locus of that ultimately to which such predications refer, or the reality that is signified in such predication. For declarations must be structured in science in that manner by which reality, in the sense assumed by that science, can indeed be implicated. For truth is simply the adequacy of language to mirror what is the case. And whether 'what is the case' is the tangible, the believable, the insightful, or the resolution of problems, depends upon the completeness of the cause used.

As indicated in our review of the topic of interpretation in Chapter 10 of our commentary on the *Nicomachean Ethics*, the primary sign of difference in the forms of interpretation is whether the reality referred to in predication lies in the phenomena of experience, or there is something else more basic on which the reality of experience depends. The manner in which a logic answers problems of interpretation reveals what that logic assumes reality to be. For the rules of interpretation shift as the nature of the real changes on which interpretation depends.

But interpretation itself is not the determination of what is real. For clearly any argument intending to prove the locus of that to which true statements refers, must itself assume that locus if it seeks to be a true argument. The question about reality thus has the same status that Kant pointed out concerning the general determination of truth, for really they are the same issue, since truth is nothing but the connection between assertion and reality.

Chapter 1. He first establishes the priorities in 'being' that exists between (1) affections, παθημάτα, of the soul, (2) things of the voice,[4] and (3) things written. For we must remember, logic is the soul's rules for defendably 'stating' things. As things written are symbols of things voiced, so these are symbols of the soul's affections, and the primary logical reality is the latter. Things written and voiced are conventions, but affections of the soul are the same to all, just as the phenomena, similar to them, are the same. The locus of the logically objective is the psychic function, not phenomena, for the locus of the logical problem is, as we said, the subject-object relation, while the relation of the soul's affections to phenomena belongs to psychology.

Few notice the differences in the use of the verb 'to assume,' τίθημι, as opposed to ὑποτίθημι or κεῖμαι or any of a half dozen others between which translators never distinguish. For what is 'assumed,' and not grasped in any other way, is a 'thesis.' It is not an hypothesis nor any other of many sorts of things present to the understanding.

Four sorts of existing things are thereby distinguished by translators, 16a3-9, (1) things written τὰ γραφόμενα, which are symbols, σύμβολα, of (2) things in the voice, τὰ ἐ τῇ φωνῇ, which in turn are symbols for (3) affections in the soul, τῶν ἐν τῇ ψυχῇ παθημάτων, which finally are the same in form as (4) the similar things, ταῦτα ὁμοιώματα πράγματα, namely the objects existing in experience. Interpretation is showing the relations stated in (1) and (2) existing by virtue of (3) and therefore (4).

But not all things uttered, φθέγγομαι,[5] are capable of being interpreted, and only some of these have the property of being

---

4. It is a patent disregard of the facts of Greek to translate φωνή, not as voice, but as sound which is the proper translation of ψόφος.

either true or false. Thus the first thing Aristotle does is to discount everything that is understood without being true or false. All the simples, therefore, grasped by the understanding, as those forming the definitions of the sciences, the 'being that was' on which demonstration is based, and what ever else is not a synthesis of reason as found in predication, is put to one side. Interpretation, then, is concerned only with the synthesizing of categories through reason and stated in arguments.

There is first of all, then, the difference between utterance that is meant to refer to an objective content, voice, and utterance that does not. For anything uttered that is neither true nor false is exempt from problems of interpretation. Truth and falsity, we remember, had nothing to do with the categories of being, for categories are not arguments. But when reason synthesizes categories to produce arguments, the synthesis either accords with what is and is thus true, or does not and is false, and is thereby capable of being interpreted. But not every synthesis of words is true or false, as 'Copperbottom' might be the name of a horse and signify something, but is not true or false. Aristotle uses the word 'goat-stag,' a fabulous animal on Eastern carpets.

Chapter 2. The ultimate link between thought and thing, which needs interpretation, is the predication or argument, λόγος, the attachment by reason, also called λόγος, of an expression, ῥῆμα, to a name, ὄνομα. Accordingly, Aristotle begins his analysis with these basic ingredients or parts of interpretation.

A name is simply a handle by which something from experience is grasped to make it manageable in thought or words, a compound of nouns, prepositions, articles, etc., that by public agreement is significant or represents some entity, no part of which is by itself significant. It can be verbally simple, like 'broom,' or verbally very complex, like 'that old fellow with the beard leaning against the pillar.' As a significance, therefore, it is

5. It is incredible how consistently the differences between sounds, ψόφοι, utterances, φθόγγοι, and voices, φωναί, is ignored.

165

elementary, a 'limit' of analysis, whatever it is verbally. When a name having a unitary significance happens to be made of otherwise separate unities, the parts no longer have the significance they had separately. He gives the word 'skiff-horse,' ἐπακτρο κέλης, meaning a skiff used by pirates, in which κέλης, meaning 'horse,' is used metaphorically, as we might talk of people 'horsing around,' and no longer has its original literal meaning.[6]

It might seem that the 'name' is the same as what is underlying, ὑποκείμενον, that he spoke of in the *Categories*, but the fact that he chose a different term in this treatise should give us pause. Scholars tell us the term ὄνομα comes from the same root, γνο, found in γιγνώσκω, to know, with the duplicated 'γ' dropped off. The term understanding, νοῦς, also comes from the same root, so they all have to do with grasping of an immediate content. It is as though Aristotle is saying, when one comes to problems of interpretation, questions of truth and falsity, one assumes one has some sort of a grasp of things. Not so when the problem is simply putting experience into bins.

The public agreement is crucial to the nature of a symbol. For the sounds of animals indeed make something evident, as the animal is hungry, wants something, etc., and this is grasped by another animal, but there is no arbitrary assignment of significance to the sound. Animal sounds are significant as thunder is significant, by having a naturally observed connection grasped by the animal, as a horse connects 'whoa' to his master's wants, but does not grasp 'whoa' as a conventional agreement, not existing by nature. Animals therefore have no awareness of names which are symbols agreed upon, but operate only by signs which are simply connections observed in experience.[7]

6. To translate this word as 'pirate-vessel,' or 'pirate-boat,' though ostensibly correct, totally obscures its metaphorical allusion, and thus obliterates the point Aristotle makes in using the example. Translation that is insensitive to the point of the text only confuses.

7. Failure to distinguish conventional symbols from natural signs leaves much discussion of animal behavior today totally confused.

Predication also involves negatings, as "What he saw was not a man," or "He saw 'not-man,'" and it is important to see, whatever the linguistic structure, logically the significance is left undetermined. Modulations of names, which in inflected languages are simply grammatical inflections, called 'fallings' by the Greeks, and which in English must be turned to awkward prepositional phrases, are also not names, for one cannot make simple assertions or denials of these as one does of names, as "Sailors exist," but "Of sailors exists" is nonsense, though in other respects they retain properties similar to names.

Chapter 3. For the soul to 'state' something, it must first grasp the topic of the statement, and this is given in the 'name,' ὄνομα. One then must grasp that which is addressed to that topic, the 'expression,' ῥῆμα. Expressions, the things attributed when predications are made of what is named, have the same properties as the names with the addition of a reference to time, as 'is,' 'was,' of 'will be.' The negation here, as in the case of names, is not an expression. For nothing has been expressed of a topic named when one says of it that it 'is not-healthy,' for there is just as much lack of expression here as before there was lack of naming with 'not-human.' Expression is something made evident, and there is no attribution given to what is represented by the name if the expression is left indefinite as it is in negation. Also, as in the case of names, one must distinguish the modulations of expressions, for past, present and future are different.

Expressions, then, by virtue of themselves, state names and signify something. With them thought takes a stand and the listener is 'arrested' by its significance. This is what makes both names and expressions take the form of limits, for they are the limit of the analysis of statement into significances. By themselves, expressions signify nothing existing or not, but need the synthesis with what is named, through reason, to accomplish this. Predicating existence thus is a function of argument or reason.

Chapter 4. The synthesis, by reason, of name and expression is argument. An argument, λόγος, is a predication, one thing of another, but the parts, separated, are only significant as saying, φάσις,[8] not as affirmation. Name and expression, by themselves, are not assertion, because they do not by themselves 'state' anything. Thus we learn that 'saying,' φάσις, is words without the logical form of argument, but still conveying significance. An argument, however, is a 'stating' that something 'is,' an expression attributed to a name. This is the difference, *Posterior Analytics* 72a14-24, between a definition, which is therefore not an argument, but can be changed into one, and an hypothesis which is already an argument. A definition becomes an affirming, or a negating, when something is added, namely the predication or withdrawal of existence, either simply or partially through an expression. The change of a definition into an argument is also discussed in the *Posterior Analytics*.

While a name or an expression is significant, the parts of them, such as a syllable, is not. Thus 'human exists' is an argument that is true or false. 'Human,' ἄνθρωπος, is a limit, either a name or an expression, and is significant. But a single syllable of human, ἄνθρωπος, such as ἄν, does not signify anything, and is only voice, φωνή. Voice is thus the material of which significances are built by convention. Voice is the intentional sound, ψόφος, made by animals, which becomes dialect, διάλεκτος, changing from sign, σημεῖν, to symbol, σύμβολον,[9] only through human convention. All these terms are constantly confused in translation, both from one treatise to another, and even within a single translation, though Aristotle is completely consistent in their use.

Argument, 16b33, is significant by agreement, not as 'organic' or instrumental. That is to say, the significances of nature are instrumentally significant in the sense that significances

8. Saying, φάσις, here as mere speech, usually means significant voice without declaration. But sometimes saying or speech includes statement, as at 21b19, so argument is a species of saying.
9. This distinction between σημεῖον and σύμβολον, carefully wrought by the Greeks, is ignored both by translators and in lexicons.

like thunder, the spores of animals, a cry of pain, or the sound of 'whoa' to a horse, are each a sign, σημεῖον, an existential, experienced, and organic relation connecting things. It is the natural connections observed between things that constitutes the significance of a sign. But a symbol, σύμβολον, is an arbitrary agreement to constitute a significance that is not a natural organic connection. Signs are the discovered significance of natural instruments, or things observed, but symbols are artificially imposed by agreements only among animals that have consciousness of their own activities, [10] and can therefore 'see' themselves, or have consciousness of themselves creating the meanings. There must be consciousness for the creation of symbols, for an animal must be conscious of itself to understand the meaning is due to its act, not to a property in things. For consciousness is the concomitant grasp of the self and the object. this is not widely understood by animal psychologists, else they would know that an animal has a language only when it teaches it to its trainer.

Arguments, however, are not all 'declarative,' ἀποφαντικός,[11] that is, they do not all attribute truth or falsity. Thus a prayer, like "May all your troubles be little ones," is an argument, but is neither true or false. The predication of an expression to a name is an argument, as here "being little ones" is expressed of something named, namely "your troubles," but the coupling states a hope not that something is true. The statements of rhetoric and poetics are all 'arguments,' for in the *Poetics*, a myth is an argu-

10. As *On the Soul* says, this occurs only with animals capable of grasping what exists by virtue of a whole, and this is possible only with animals who are conscious, συνειδέναι, not with those who have merely perceptual awareness, συναισθάνομαι, as the *Nicomachean Ethics* distinguishes these.

11. To translate ἀπόφανσις as 'proposition,' as both Edghill and Cooke do, rather than 'declaration,' is unfortunate, for the arguments of rhetoric and poetics do indeed 'propose' something, but they do not 'declare' or 'establish' anything, for proposing is laying something out for consideration or establishment.

ment, but they are not the sort to which truth and falsity are relevant. Inquiry is concerned, then, only with declarative arguments, for logic 'establishes' statements, poetry does not.

Chapter 5. An argument is a declaration, ἀπόφανσις, concerning something either as an affirming, κατάφασις, or as a negating, ἀπόφασις.[12] These words all derive from the root term φαίνω, which mean 'to bring to light,' and are the irreducible ultimate units of argument or reasoning. All other arguments are simply compounds, or 'things bound together,' out of these. A declarative argument is thus one either because it makes one thing evident, or because it is the binding together of many such arguments. When the predicate is stated 'by virtue of' what underlies, not accidentally 'of' what underlies, the unity lies in the fact that the predicate is already contained in what underlies. The unity of an extended argument like the *Physics* is the binding of such elemental arguments on the basis of its principle.

Therefore, 17a17, name and expression are only 'saying,' φάσις,[13] for shedding light is not necessarily asserting. Neither a name nor an expression is thus either itself a declaration when one initiates the talking, or an answer to a question when asked by someone else, for even if we verbally give only one, the other part has been implied in the question or answer.

We handle experience by connecting a name, ὄνομα, with an expression, ῥῆμα, attempting to mirror the connections discovered in experience. I have not been able as yet to establish the

12. All these terms are used throughout the corpus of Aristotle precisely as he here defines them, and therefore should be translated suitably to what he says here.

13. Mere speech, something spoken without affirming or asserting anything. Many of these terms, as in the case of φάσις, are badly confused in lexicons. The range for a given word is not often determined from a few uses only, where many meanings may in fact 'work.' The use of a word in other treatises should be compared, for Aristotle's language is uniform throughout the body of his writings. He does not vacillate as our translators and lexicons do.

fact, but I am willing to wager a fair sum that the name for Hermes (Latin Mercury) Ἑρμῆς is derived from the word to speak or express ἐρῶ, for all that is lacking is the aspirate. This would make interpretation the discovering of expressions that can be legitimately connected with what has been named. The main distinction between ὄνομα and ῥῆμα is then the distinction between what is grasped by the understanding and what is asserted by reason, for predication is the function of reason λόγος. But no commentator or translator of Greek thought to date has understood the functional difference between these two intellectual functions, that understanding is 'seeing' the principles of science, while reason is 'knowing,' through cause, the attributes demonstrated in science. As ὄνομα comes from the same root as γνο found in γιγνώσκω, to know, so ἐρῶ (the etymological source of ῥῆμα), in contrast, comes from the same root, ἐρ, found in ἔρομαι, to ask, and from its future or aorist ῥήτωρ, comes rhetorician. It is the difference between a sort of divine reception of what is given and the attachment to it of something else, also divinely given, but the attachment being a function of human reason. Liddell and Scott even suggest that ῥῆμα comes from ῥέω, to flow, so that the expression is the flowing of the name, the abiding becoming what moves, and of course it is not the divine that flows.

Chapter 6. This chapter defines what is meant by a contradiction, ἀντίφασις, namely the opposition, ἀντικειμένον, of two declarations, one an affirming the other a negating, stating the same thing (the expression) of the same thing (the name), with no change in the entities stated.[14]

Chapter 7. But there are other relations between declarations, for besides being either positive or negative, declarations

14. It must be noticed that contradiction is a relation only between arguments, while simples can be contrary. Thus in Greek the prefix ἀντί and in English the prefix contra, and in both the root 'to say.' The word does not appear in the Categories.

also differ in that what is attributed or not is attributed of what is either by virtue of a whole or particular. In current translations Aristotle's meaning is subverted because this distinction between whole and part turns into a statistical difference between all and some. This is because the phrase "what is naturally predicated of many," ὃ ἐπὶ πλειόνων πέφυκε κατηγορεῖσθαι has not been understood. When something is naturally predicated, the predicate is part of the nature of what underlies. The predication is therefore by virtue of a whole, of a thing as such, by virtue of what it is, not simply of 'all' things that happen to be of a sort. For if the predicate is true, not only of 'all' of that sort, but others as well, it is not true of that thing naturally or by virtue of a whole. But in Edghill and Cooke the phrase has been interpreted to mean only that it is the nature of the predicate to be predicated either of all or many things, and the 'nature' turns out to be that of the predicate rather than the object of which it is predicated. By this error a functional relation, something being predicated by virtue of a whole because it is a part of the nature of that whole, is turned into a statistical relation of something whose nature happens to make it applied to things of a certain name. The effect is thus the same here as in the failure at other places to properly translate the preposition κατά, and the very basis of demonstrative science is lost, a pivotal error. It is what happens when a translator, using a reductive procedure, fails to understand Aristotle's functional logical relations.

What is first brought up as by virtue of whole or part is that of which the predication is made, the underlying thing. But there is also a difference in the predication itself being by virtue of whole or part. When both the underlying thing of which the predication is made, and the predication itself, exist by virtue of a whole, but the attribution is either affirmative or negative, the result is two declarations that are opposed as contraries, as "All men are white" and "No humans are white." In these both the object of which the predication is made, human, and the predication made of human, exist by virtue of a whole. Declarations then are contrary when everything else remains the same and the only difference is that between affirming and negating.

But when the object of which the predication is made is by virtue of a whole, but the predication is not, the declarations are no longer contraries. In the declarations "Human is white" and "Human is not-white" the object of which the predication is made, human, is still by virtue of a whole, but the predication is not made by virtue of a whole, for it is not of all humans that the predication is made. These two statements are not contraries of each other because they can be simultaneously true. This illustrates the importance of the difference between the negation of a term in a declaration and the negation of the declaration. When logic is interpreted as merely statistical relations, this functional difference is completely lost. It was in order to make such distinctions that Aristotle first carefully defined name and expression, and then the argument of which they are parts, for both parts and whole can be either by virtue of a whole or partial.

Having shown that whole and part can apply either to the object of which the predication is made, or to the predicating itself, Aristotle then turns to the third factor, the predicate, 17b12-16. This he shows must always be partial,[15] for no proposition wholy predicates a whole of a whole, as "All men are all animals." That this matter is indeed a question of functional wholes, and not a matter of statistics, is easily seen in this case, for predications and sophistical equations are not the same.

It is by means of such distinctions, then, that Aristotle is able to define contradiction, ἀντίφασις. For an affirming, κατάφασις, is contradictory, not contrary, to a negating, ἀπόφασις, when the predication, of the same thing, is in one case by virtue of a whole and in the other case not. Thus, "All men are white" is contradicted by "Not all men are white," and "No men are white"[16] is contradicted by "Some men are white."

15. What logic now statistically calls undistributed.
16. The Greek literally says "Not one human is white."

As stated at 17b3 when affirming and negating are both by virtue of a whole the relation is that of contrariety, as "All men are just" and "No men are just," and so cannot both be simultaneously true. But the two declarations opposed to these are not contraries, but can be simultaneously true, as "Not all men are white" and "Some men are white."

Of a contradiction, by virtue of a whole, of what is by virtue of a whole, one part must be true, the part false, and so also of particulars. But when the predication is not made by virtue of a whole, but is made indefinitely, as "Human is white" and "Human is not white," this does not hold, for both can be true. This will then show that the common sense notion that "Human is not white" signifies that "No human is white" is false. For the first allows the possibility that "Some humans are white," but the second does not. There is also one affirming for each negating, for the negating denies what the affirming asserts and as the affirming asserts it.

Thus from the primitive notions of negating and affirming, Aristotle has defined contradictory and contrary declarations, and it is these specific meanings that hold throughout Aristotle's writings, though few translators consistently translate accordingly, and as a consequence opposites, contraries and contradictions often become quite confused.

Chapter 8. The unities of predication in speech are the effect of the unities in existing things. What allows the unity of substance to be reproduced in predication is the fact that the predication in science is always 'by virtue of' what underlies, and this is why correct translation is so very important. Aristotle is careful to stipulate that declarations are one when they signify "one thing stated by virtue of one thing," not 'one thing said of one thing.' For there is no unity to something merely said about one thing, as that 'the book is on the table.' Accidental attributions yield no unities. Only when the predicate has the authority of the thing of which it is predicated, when it is predicated 'by virtue of' that underlying thing, when the predication is natural, is there any unity. Yet such exactness is lacking in both the Oxford and Loeb translations, as well as in all modern statistical thinking, which reduces all functional 'unities' to such statistical 'unities' as Russell's 'class' of red objects.

Aristotle, in fact, goes on to state in principle precisely this point, for giving one word to two things does not make them a unity. This of course is precisely what is done in statistics, and is what Russell is doing in calling red things a class. As a result, Aristotle concludes, with such 'unities' the dictum about contradictions will not hold. The consequences are far flung.

Chapter 9. The generalizations so far made have been expressly concerned, as we have noted, with predications made by virtue of a whole concerning what is by virtue of a whole. In other words, the statements have been restricted to matters of the contemplative sciences. But there is also science that is concerned with particulars, and the case of particulars is quite different. If the dictum that every declaration is either true or false is taken as valid for every declaration, there are absurd consequences. For example, if a predictive contradiction arises, one person saying something will arise, another denying exactly that attribution, a literal interpretation of the dictum, stating one or the other part of any contradiction is true, will state that before the attribution occurs, one part is true, the other false. For it is not possible to attribute both parts of a contradiction. Such a literal interpretation of the dictum will then have the absurd consequences of making an attribution true before it even comes to be, and will also make whatever will be exist of necessity, for it will then be possible to say it could not 'not-be.' For, at 18a39, if it is true to express that X is either Y or not Y, then it must be necessary that X be either Y or not Y, and if X is either Y or not Y, either to say X is Y or to deny X is Y must be true. And with this interpretation of the dictum, as universally applicable, of every contradictory affirming and negating, whether of what is by virtue of a whole, or of what is particular, whatever the time either of the attribution or of the statement about the attribution, one or the other is necessarily true.

The implications of this, of course, is that nothing exists by chance or is contingent upon human choice, but everything exists only of necessity. For if a contingent truth is interpreted to be true eternally, before the contingency produces it, it ceases to be a contingency. All practical inquiry is thus swept away with this one dictum, "Che sera sera," taken literally to apply to all declarations. For if what will be will be even before it exists, there is no point to deliberation and making any undertaking, 18b31-2, this distinction clearly reflecting the difference between the practical and the productive. And though Aristotle quite adamantly says, at 18b38-39, that it is not because of the human act of affirming or denying that makes things whatever way they will be, still, as we saw, the truth of the statement implies or rests on a truth concerning reality. For truth is a relation between what is stated and the nature of reality.

But at 19a7 Aristotle says "these things are unable to be," not impossible, but unable to be. That is, the impossibility of their being derives from the lack of power in the thing itself, not from any external preventing circumstance, for that is the difference between what is impossible, τὸ μὴ ἐνδεχόμενον, and what is unable, τὸ ἀδύνατον, though the distinction is ignored by translators. What is important at this point is to discover Aristotle's argument that shows this. For it is the argument which teaches us, not the conclusion.

The reason, he says at 19a7 is that the principle of what is to be comes from both deliberating and doing, that in general what is able to be (not what is possible) exists in things that are not always in activity. And to things that have the power (are able) both to be and not, both being and not being are possible.[17] It is therefore the principle of the practical that assures us of the existence of contingency, and as the *Nicomachean Ethics* argued, Book I, Chapter 1, the principle of the practical is the

17. 'What is able to be' is thus part of 'what is possible of being.'

176

end, and as Book I, Chapter 2, showed, this is a reflexive notion that is the warrant of its own existence, as are all principles.[18] The argument in sum is that the principle of the practical is shown to exist because its dialectical defense shows there is no ground upon which its negating can be based, and any possible position in respect of the practical necessarily assumes it.

We are thereby, 19a18, constrained, as inquirers of objective experience, to affirm the existence of some things as based on other principles than necessity. This means that prior to the actuality of the potentiality, neither the affirming nor the negating is more true in respect of any declaration concerning a particular. Whatever exists, therefore, exists whenever it exists, and does not exist whenever it does not, and declarations to be true must reflect this.

This then, is Aristotle's provision for the existential basis of the particular. Without this distinction between the fashion in which declarations about particulars are interpreted and the fashion is which declarations concerning what exist by virtue of a whole are interpreted, there would be no autonomy to the particular, and the dependence of what is by virtue of a whole upon the priority of the particular could not be articulated. The chapter is thus critical to Aristotle's phenomenalist interpretation, and the philosophic positions against which he labors here, are those McKeon calls ontic. For if what exists by virtue of a whole, whether ideas as in Plato, or elements as in Democritus, is prior in being to the particular, these relationships between expression and name in the formation of arguments are radically altered.

Chapter 10. An affirmation is an expression stated 'by virtue of' either a name or a non-name, i.e. an indefinite name. Thus "All birds fly" predicates flying of what is named 'bird,' while "No bird breathes under water" predicates breathing under water of the indefinite name no-bird, because what 'is' signified is not

18. This matter is extensively examined in our commentary on the *Nicomachean Ethics*, Chapter 10.

defined. If the expression is made indefinite, as in "All birds are not six-legged," no affirmation is effected. This clearly puts different functional limitations on expressions and names, quite apart from the difference in respect of the indication of time.

Expressions have been distinguished in themselves from names by their indication of time. Later, in the *Prior Analytics*, the examination of the syllogism requires treating the expression and name as the same by removing the reference to time in the expression. When they are treated the same they are called limits. They are called limits because they are the limit of the logical analysis of arguments into their parts. The same content can then be interchanged in a declaration to form either a predicate or the underlying thing of which the predication is made. The element of time separated from the expression then becomes a third thing, a mere coupling between the limits. This eradication of any difference between the two allows for the sort of calculative procedures that are followed in the *Analytics*. The procedure happens also to be the one extended universally to all science in the logistic method. It is the separated 'is' of the expression that he refers to at 19b19 as being a third thing, as in "X is Y," where X and Y are 'limits' of discourse coupled by 'is.'

When a declaration is viewed as the coupling of two limits by the verb 'is,' it is then easy to see whether what is negated is one of the limits or the coupling between them. The problem appeared before, at 17b3, in distinguishing between a name stated by virtue of a whole and a prediction stated by virtue of a whole. The logic of the square of opposition is then easy to read, as we have printed it in our translation. Two of the four are negations of the coupling, shown by the difference between 'is' and 'is-not,' two are negations of the limit, shown by the difference between 'just' and 'not-just,' making the square a total of four, or two times two.

One square is made with the predication not by virtue of a whole, at 19b27, p.49, another with the predication by virtue of a whole, at 19b33. But the logic relations between the four change in the second case. A third square results from making the limit that underlies indefinite, at 19b38, both on p.50. This exhausts the possible antitheses.

In Greek, as in English, the logical structure of the declarative statement is sometimes not only not abetted by the structure of common language, but is often seriously compromised. One must then structure the common declaration to conform with logical intent. This is the sort of advice by Aristotle that is ignored by those seeking to derive his metaphysical notions from the customary structure of the Greek language. The rest of the chapter is devoted to similar details necessary to the structuring of logical language. For common language grew in a system that responded to immediate practicalities which only turned from short range to longer range as the understanding of men also grew. Truth was never an immediately understood value, and therefore the structuring of language to meet this end has been, with every conceivable philosophic or scientific procedure, a continuous problem. This is why the charge that anyone could structure his philosophy on the basis of common linguistic distinctions could only be made by a simple mind.

Chapter 11. Aristotle here turns to the problem of the unity of a declarative statement. For there is little to chose between saying that a declaration is true and saying that it forms a unity, since no falsity forms a unity. This is why the *Metaphysics* says that what is one has as many meanings as what exists. Therefore, if one statement is about one thing the unity of the statement must be the reproduction in the statement of the unity of the thing. But if a scientific predication exists 'by virtue of' what underlies the predication, the unity of the declaration depends primarily on the unity of the entities or limits signified in those predications. It is then seen that the unities determined in the *Categories* provide for the possibility of unities in predication.

For it is possible in common language to assign one word for a assemblage of things that have no unity, as in Russell's logic, and as a result the declaration in which it appears has only the appearance of unity. In Aristotle's examples at 20b16, 'animal, two-footed and tame' are one because from these predicates one thing arises. But from 'white, human, and walking,' 20b18, no one thing arises. What he means is that with these three predicates one gets three different groups designating different, though perhaps overlapping, groups of particulars, so that whatever has any one of these predicates does not have all three as well. There is nothing, therefore, that 'by virtue of' its being precisely that which is named, as when all three predicates are predicated through one word, is as claimed. In other words, the underlying object stated is fictitious. The voice, then, may be one, but the defendable predications are three, not one.

This detailed explanation, incidentally, reveals the absolute necessity for translating κατά, not simply by the genitive case, as 'of,' but by the phrase 'by virtue of,' for the whole of science as determined by Aristotle's procedure, depends on the fact that the warrant of the predicate is found in the nature of what is designated as the underlying thing. This is what makes the procedure of the entire *Organon* analytic. For the predication depends upon the term, and the syllogism depends upon the predication. If this is not assumed in all predication, but predication is seen to be simply anything that might momentarily hold of a object, and not the object as such, the only basis of science is a statistical analysis in which all control of predication through the interfunctioning of things is lost. This is because the things they are about are chaotically defined, and the dependency of the being of one thing upon another has been lost. A statistical analysis of an area of investigation is always a sign that inquirers find the fact highly confusing, for they do not know the things they discuss well enough to predicate accurately, in more than a nominal way, what is entailed by what. When statistics, then, is exalted as the most basic procedure of science, the inquirer has simply agreed with the ancient sophists, that reality does not abide, all things flow, and nothing named stands still long enough to be known.

A statistical analysis, which Aristotle is cautioning us against, and which is the implementation of the mode of thought which McKeon called discrimination, thus drastically narrows the range of inquiry, for it precludes a functional exploration of facts, while the functional analysis finds a valid but ancillary place for relatively unorganized statistical material. Its place is in history, the propaedeutic to science that gathers fact, τὸ ὅτι, which science turns from what is 'seen' to what is 'known,' by discovering the functional why, τὸ διότι, or cause. It can do this only through the careful articulation of the entities it talks about, and makes all its predications 'by virtue of' what underlies. For the cause can be precisely known only when the experienced fact has been properly categorized, as limit, and when any predication is 'by virtue of' that of which it is predicated.

This explication of the difference between the statistical procedure of discrimination and Aristotle's will illustrate why, in our final chapter on Aristotle's *On the Soul*, we said that the different procedures cannot be simply dismissed as historically they have been, as false or invalid, for each does indeed what it claims to do if we see accurately what it is they claim. But they can be distinguished in terms of other virtues. The one that we pointed out there is that each procedure either relinquishes accuracy and precision to achieve wider applicability, or the later for the former. Their virtues are thus a function of their vices, or vice versa if that is more acceptable.

The topic at 20b22 then turns to the originating of such declarations, for in some sciences they come from the dialectic which produces the primary premises of a science. For there is no more accuracy in the conclusion than there is in the first premises. It is clear that if in a dialectical questioning, one is asked what is it that is 'white, human, and walking' the answer would have to be many since the questions, though disguised, are many. But it is also evident that in some sciences the search for the 'what it is' which produces not only the essence or 'the being that was,' but also the properties of the things whose demonstration forms a good part of the science of the thing, the procedure cannot be dialectical. This is because, unlike the procedure that searches for the best of commonly held opinions, the 'what it is' of any contemplative science is determined, not by choosing between alternatives offered, but by inspection of the facts as recounted in the beginning of the *Metaphysics* and the close of the *Posterior Analytics*. If therefore the questioner does not offer the precision that accords with the facts, the one answering is unable to answer.

The question at 20b31 then is when do multiple predications form a unity? Some things predicated separately can be predicated in conjunction because they do form a unity, like animal and two-footed of human. So also with human and white. But good and shoemaker do not form such a unity.

First, at 21a7, both predicates (as whiteness), and the things of which they are predicated (as that which is white),[19] that are stated accidentally, either when each is stated of the same thing or when they are stated of each other, do not make a unity. For no accidental relation is a unity. Secondly, predicates do not make a unity if one inheres in, ἐνυπάρχω, another (as white inheres in what is white), and thereby a predicate must state what inheres in the underlying object, without inhering in what inheres, as white is predicated of both human and white human and therefore is not properly predicated. This is obvious, for then the predication is not 'by virtue of' what underlies, if what underlies can be either of two things. Thus if white is predicated both of human and of a white human, it is not predicated by virtue of what underlies. The criterion, he says at 21a21, is if a contradiction arises as one adds attributes and an attribute contradicts the previous attributes, then the attribution is falsely made, as calling a dead human a human.

Chapter 12. The unity of a declarative statement was stated generally, deriving the unity of the predication, in Aristotle's language, from the attribution of the predicate by virtue of what

19. A distinction noted by Aristotle but ignored by translators.

underlies, or in modern idiom, from the essential relation of the predicate to the subject. Modern logic, however, not only ignores that problem, because it sees the affairs of science conducted statistically on the basis of no functional distinctions between entities discussed, but also ignores in the main the next problem, the distinction between the 'manner' or 'turn,' τρόπος given to the 'existence' of the predication.

But Aristotle's procedure necessitates a distinction between what is able to exist, δύναμαι, what is possible of existing, ἐνδέχομαι, and what necessarily exists, ἐξ ἀνάγκη εἶναι. In a statistical approach such distinctions have a minimum of importance, and therefore often dismissed. In previous translations these three are not uniformly translated and one cannot be sure of what the Greek is saying, for the first might be translated 'can' or 'able' or 'may be' or 'possible,' the second as 'may be' or 'contingent' or 'possible,' and the third as 'necessary' or 'must be,' etc., so that not only is it impossible to understand from the translation that the same idea is involved, but one cannot even tell which of the three, if one knew there were three, might be referred to at any point. We believe ours is the first translation in English, and perhaps in any language, to translate them uniformly and differently so they may be distinguished. In certain contexts the distinction is critical, in some there is no visible difference in function. But unless translated differently and consistently in every case, the reader will not know the contextual difference.

The point that Aristotle is most concerned with establishing is that the relationship between predicate and what underlies in these different 'modes' of predication yields quite different oppositions between declarations, and the rules of predication therefore change in important ways. We are to examine or look at, σκοπέω, the facts, τὸ ὅτι, not to investigate, ἐπισκοπέω, or inquire into the why, τὸ διότι, concerning the relations of affirmings and negatings, in each of these 'modes' or manners of being. Logic is an analysis of that for which we might search, ζητέω, as given in experience, but it is not by inquiring, ἐπιζητέω,[20] for causes as in science. The first listing he gives of them puts them into two pairings, first distinguishing things able to be and unable to be from things possible and not possible, then distinguishing matters concerning what is unable and what is necessary. Clearly he would not set things up this way if there was no difference between what is able to be and what is possible.

We are looking, among things 'put together,' συντιθέμενον, or 'woven together,' συμπλοκή, by human reason, which is the faculty that makes predications or attributions or declarations, for understanding grasps immediate signifcances only, for differences in the oppositions afforded by these different manners of predication. Among the relations between such predications, the most basic, from which we start as the given topic, is that of contradiction, ἀντιφασις, 'saying what is anti.' This relation he says is 'ordered' by virtue of 'the being' and 'the not being,' of the same things. We have here the first separation, in its analysis, of a predication into two limits coupled by an assertion in respect of being, three parts instead of the two with which the treatise started. The relation of contradiction is asserted not to involve the limits or entities of this predication in three parts, but simply to change the coupling, asserting either is or is not. Since this is the interpretation of predication that must be used to produce the logistic calculations of the syllogism in the *Analytics*, it is crucial to see it employed here in the *Concerning Interpretation*, where the discussion has first turned on the relation between an expression, ῥῆμα, and a name, ὄνομα, with the coupling absorbed by the expression. For this establishes that the difference in interpretation is extrinsic to the nature of the thing.

The contradictory relation between affirming and negating he first illustrates with indefinite declarations, as the negating of 'human is white' is 'human is-not white,' where the negating is of the coupling, not a negating of the predicate as in 'human is not-

20. Compare footnote 29, page 59 above. There seems to be no end to the subtleties and precisions of the Greeks.

white.' He proves this by showing that if it were held to be the latter, since wood is not-human, stating the declarations by virtue of a whole, rather than indefinitely, as in 'all humans are not-white,' wood would be not-white human. This also illustrates his procedure, for analysis discovers the implications of what is assumed through the avoidance of contradiction.

If then there are predications with other couplings, such as 'is able to be,' 'is possible,' or 'is necessary,' those couplings replacing the 'is' must perform the same function. The separation of the coupling in this way is what enables us to observe what is negated, for it is the failure to observe this that confuses the relations between declarations. If the negating of 'what is human walks' is not 'what is not-human walks,' but 'what is human walks-not,' then by analogous structure it would seem, at 21b10, that the negating of 'what is able to be' is not 'what is not able to be' but 'what is able to not-be.' For it would appear that, as in the first example, we have simply negated the predicate.

The rebuttal is a point of fact, that the two arguments are both able to be, though not simultaneously. But statements that are opposed in respect of the same thing are not able both to be true, as this interpretation would have it. We then have a choice between insisting that in contradiction the same thing is stated and denied of the same thing, or insisting that the addition of being and not being brings about statements and denials.[21] Since the first is shown to be unable to be, we pick the second. By this we discover that the negating in a contradiction is a negating of the coupling, not a negating of the predicate. The denial of 'what is able to be' is then 'what is not able to be' and not 'what is able to not-be.' The contradictions concerning the other modes are the same. And the rest of the chapter runs through the various contradictions, ending with two lists of oppositions.

Chapter 13. From these assumptions there are logical con-

21. It is apparent that there is some problem with the text here concerning negations, but Aristotle's intentions remain clear.

sequences. Aristotle first notes consequences between these two lists, that 'what is possible to be' is consequential to 'what is able to be,' and that these turn about. Then at 22a16 he notes that these two also turn about with two in the second list, 'what is not unable to be' and 'what is not necessary to be.' This reciprocal character, however, has been misconstrued. Translators have assumed that it means there is no difference between 'what is possible to be' and 'what is able to be,' and they may therefore be translated indifferently. But though being unable (i.e. the lack in the thing itself of the potentiality for the action) implicates the impossibility of the action generally, and though the impossibility of the action generally implicates the inability of the thing to perform the action, such implications in no way make what is able and what is possible the same. They are still different, for mutual implication can hold only between different things.

He then notes at 22a17 other relations beyond his lists, that suggest that his lists must be expanded by negations, not only to the predications, but to the entities predicated. He therefore draws up four sets of declarations, consisting of what is able, possible, unable, and necessary, to display the consequences between them. The four sets display these predications first (1) in their original affirmative form, then (2) with only the coupling negated, which as we know from Chapter 6 results in the contradiction of the original declaration, and then below these, (3) with the predicate only negated and finally (4) with both the coupling and the predicate negated. This is the only diagrammatic rendering of statements in the text as it is given us. In the editing nothing is stated as to the arrangement of the original sources. Other diagrams are drawn by some translators, but the text we are given in such cases, as at 22a11, is cursive, not diagrammatic.

The consequences noted at 22a17 that led to setting up the four sets, which can now be better seen by virtue of the diagram, are first, that the declarations of the third set, 'what is not necessary not to be' and 'what is not unable not to be,' are consequent to 'what is able not to be' and 'what is possible not to be' in the

186

same set, and at 22a19 that 'what is necessary not to be' and 'what is unable to be' from the second set are consequent to 'what is not able to be' and 'what is not possible to be' in the same set.

The question to be asked is what is the difference between the consequences seen in the first two lists, not diagramed, and the consequences that led to and can be seen only in the four diagramed sets? The first two lists were constructed verbally, not logically, for the first list took all the affirmative predications, the second took their negations or contradictions. But when the list were examined they proved not to be logically homogeneous. To obtain the logical relations between these propositions it was necessary to forget the accidents of common speech and list predications, not in terms of the presence or absence of linguistic signs of affirmation and negation, but in terms of the logical relations between expressions and names, found by explication of the things referred to. For the connecting terms like 'necessary' proved to have complicated logical relations to the other connecting terms. Let us then look at what constitutes the similarity of those in a set. The logic obviously centers on the first.

'What is possible' is obviously reciprocal to 'what is able.' Then since 'what is unable' is the contrary to 'what is able,' it would seem that its opposite, 'what is not unable,' must be consonant to 'what is able.' And since 'what is necessary' certainly is not 'what is able,' it seems at least at first blush that what is able is not what is necessary. Thus the sets of four appear to be what common sense would lump together as appearing without closer scrutiny to belong together. They are then not final commitments, but simply first approximations, looking like common sense.

The scrutiny starts by first noting, at 22a32, that 'what is unable' (or 'what is not able to be') in set 2 is contradictorily consequent to 'what is possible' and 'what is able' in set 1, and 'what is not unable' in set 1 is contradictorily consequent to 'what is not possible' and 'what is not able' in set 2, and in a

187

reciprocal way. This will be the standard that sets the problem, and it is when other considerations are compared to this and found wanting that problems emerge.

At 22a38, then, he turns to 'what is necessary' to see if the same consequences hold. One would expect the denial of 'what is necessary not to be' in set 2 to be 'what is not necessary to be' in set 1, just as the denial of 'what is unable to be' in set 2 is 'what is able to be' in set 1, but it is not, for both may be true of the same thing. The reason why they are not, he says, at 22b3, is that 'what is unable' is rendered contrarily to 'what is necessary,' though having the same force. Thus if it is unable to be, it is necessary that it not be, as in set 2. And if it is unable not to be, it is necessary to be, as in set 4. In these two cases the declarations using 'unable' (on the pattern of declarations using 'able) find consequences in contrary declarations using 'necessary. And so far it seems that 'what is necessary' and 'what is unable' are reciprocally contrary to each other.

But, at 22b10, it seems that the contradictories of what is necessary[22] are not able to have this consequence to what is unable. This is because what is necessary is also what is able to be, yet by the rule given above 'what is necessary' has as its conse-

22. Both Edghill and Cook sprinkle their translations with awkward and meaningless Britishisms that thoroughly complicate what is already a difficult subject just from a verbal point of view. To take a straightforward expression like 'what is necessary' at 22b17 and turn it into 'what is necessary that it should be,' with a repetition of 'that it should' for each occurrence of 'necessary' in very complicated sentences, is alone a fearful obstacle to be hurdled every few words, even after one has discovered that, despite the customary meaning of 'should,' the translator, in using the idiosyncrasies of his social class, is not attempting to mix normative issues into logical ones. To read 'it is possible that it should be' when Aristotle says simply 'it is possible' is a garrulous affectation, a vacuous addition lending no clarity and great cacophony. For one is continually diverted from what Aristotle is saying by the instinctive inclination to regard 'it is necessary that it should be' as a normative requirement, rather than an alternative logical structure.

quence the contrary, namely 'what is unable to be,' which is absurd. Yet even though what is necessary is what is able to be, still, 22b17, what is able to be is not necessary. But what is necessary not to be is also not consequent to what is able to be, for what is able to be may either be or not. Therefore, 22b22, what is not necessary not to be is a consequence of what is able to be, and this (what is not necessary not to be) is equally true by virtue of what is necessary to be. The reason for this is that 'what is not necessary not to be' is the contradiction of 'what is necessary not to be' which is the consequence of 'what is not able to be.' The result, 22b27, is that the contradictories of 'what is necessary' have these uniquenesses and when explicated in this way result in nothing that is unable to be, however surprising.

The close following of Aristotle's argument concerning the peculiarities of these logical oppositions is difficult and tedious. We have not found there is any possibility of simplifying Aristotle's argument while preserving both its force and accuracy. We have attempted therefore merely to state it in a different way in order to articulate what he is doing.

There is still, however, the possibility of a problem as to whether 'what is able to be' does indeed follow 'what is necessary.' If it does not follow its contradictory, 'what is not able to be,' must, or if not that, then 'what is able not to be.' But both of these are false by virtue of 'what is necessary,' the assumption from which we started. Since it is the same thing that is both able to be cut and not cut, able to be and not be, it might seem that it is the same thing is both necessary to be and possible of not being, but this is false. For what is necessary to be is not possible of not being. The conclusion then, 22b36, is that not everything that is able (either to be, to walk or whatever) has the ability of the opposite. At 22b38, he first considers things whose activity does not involve reason, like fire, which is able to heat but is not able to do the opposite. Powers (abilities) that are accompanied by reason are indeed potential of contraries, like good and evil, doing or not, and this is true of some powers that are irrational. But not all potentialities existing by virtue of the lack of reason possess opposite potentialities, even when they are stated by virtue of the same form. Some potentialities are homonymously named, 23a6, that is, the same word is given them, but they are given other arguments so the word is ambiguous. Some things are able, or are potentialities, in the sense that the potentiality exists in activity. One is able to walk because one walks. We state that the thing is able because in fact it performs that ability. But other things we state to be able, not because it does the activity, but because it might do it. Thus a baby that has never walked is able to walk because it might walk. Or a human that has no science is able to know because he has faculties by which that science might be learned. Which sort of potentiality, then is consequent to something that is necessary, in the sense that what is necessary must also be able to be? Obviously only the first potentiality is consequent to what is necessary. For nothing can be necessary of which the potentiality is itself only potential.

The logical consequence of this limitation of the consequences of what is necessary is that what exists of necessity exists in actuality and not merely potentially. And though of any actuality one can say it is a potentiality of the thing, or what the thing is able, a potentiality of what is necessary is always actualized, and does not exist as a potential. Therefore, if eternal things are prior, activity is also prior to potentiality, for the potentiality in any case depends for its existence upon the activity.

In the end there are three possible attributions. Some things, as primary substances,[23] such as god and the heavenly bodies, are activities and are never merely potential. Some things are activities with potentialities, which though later in time, are prior in being to the potentialities. Some things are never activities, but always remain potentialities.

Chapter 14. The final problem is whether in the case of

23. It is conceded by all, primary substances here means, not individually existing things, as at 2a35, but eternal substances.

declarations, not limits or entities understood as in the *Categories*, but the predications formed by reason out of these limits, whether the contrary of an affirming is a negating or another affirming. In other words, what is the contrary of a λόγος, 23a28, not the contrary of an ὅρος, 6b15 and 10b12. Aristotle's problem is formulated with precisely this distinction, for he asks, if vocal matters are consequent to things that are thought, is an opinion contrary because the entity it concerns is itself contrary, the argument as a result of the limit. For already we know that while relatives and qualities have contraries, as cited above, substances and quantities do not, as stated at 3b24 and 5b11. Though he doesn't mention it, it would follow that if the contrariety of the argument was based on the contrariety of the predicate, then declarations about substances and quantities would have no contrary. The contrary to 'Kallias is just,' if the contrariety of the predicate determines the contrariety of the declaration, would be 'Kallias is unjust,' for 'just' and 'unjust' are contrary limits. But if this relation between limits and arguments does not hold, then perhaps the contrary of 'Kallias is just' is 'Kallias is-not just,' with the negation being of the predication rather than the predicate.

He starts by assuming the truth of the declaration that 'the good is good' and the falsehood of the statement that 'the good is not-good,' with the predicate being replaced by its contrary. The question then is whether the contrary of the original declaration is this or that 'the good is evil.' And if 'the not-good' and 'the evil' are the same, by virtue of which is the contrary declaration produced.

Because the opinion that the good is good and the evil is evil are both true and perhaps even the same opinion, and yet the declarations are of contraries, it is obvious that changing limits to their contraries does not produce contrary declarations. Therefore, it is not by being concerned with contraries that arguments are contrary to one another. Contrary predications are contrary, 23b7, by the contrary way in which the predication is made, in other words by the negation of the copula.

To support this claim he then says, suppose there be an opinion of the good that it is good and another that it is not good. Suppose there are also other opinions about the good that attribute to the good what is not attributable to it, or that do not attribute what is attributable, both of which go to infinity. We must only assume that the contrary is among the things in which there is deception, for the contrary of the true must be false. Contraries are also the things from which geneses arise, for things come to be something or the contrary. Deception therefore arises from opposites as genesis does.

Then, comparing the two declarations, 'the good is good' and 'the good is not evil,' the first concerns what exists 'by virtue of itself,' while the second concerns what exists 'by virtue of an accident.' For it merely 'happens' that good is not evil because it 'happens' that evil is the contrary of good. What is true of a thing 'by virtue of what it is' is more true of it than 'what is true of it 'by virtue of an accident.' But the same thing must be said of the false, that what is more false is what is false 'by virtue of what it is.' Therefore, the denial that the good is good is more false than the falsity of the affirming that the good is evil. But the one who is most completely false about any matter, 23b21, is one who holds the opinion that is contrary to the truth, for about the same thing it is contraries that differ the most. Therefore, if of two opinions concerning the same thing the one that is concerned with the contradiction is more contrary, then since the contradiction of 'the good is good' is 'the good is not good,' this contradiction is the contrary. The opinion that 'the good is evil' actually involves two steps of reason, first that evil is not-good, and then the concluding declaration that 'the good is evil.'

Several things are significant about Aristotle's argument concerning the contrary. One is the necessity of determining what it is, entity or argument, of which the contrary is sought, for things, we have seen are contrary as well as predications of things. Second, is that contrary arguments presuppose the nature of contradictions. Third, that the articulation of the contrary presupposes the distinction between substance and accident. The whole argument is thus incompetent to a sophistical approach to science making fundamental the statistical formulation of fact. Rather like using a hammer to open a can of beans.

At 23b27 he turns to problems about universalizing this claim. As noted, some limits have contraries, as relatives and qualities, but some do not, as substances and how much. The example given has been one from quality. Where the entity or limit has no contrary, as human has no contrary since he is a substance, the false opinion is simply the opposite of the true, and that 'human is not human' is such an opposite. But this has precisely the verbal structure already affirmed as the contrary argument. Therefore, the claim is supported by its generalization to all forms of predicates. What is interesting is which of the two procedures is considered by Aristotle to be primary, and which merely auxiliary. The order exists because the second only shows the possibility of general application. It is the first that gives the answer as necessary to the nature of the thing. The distinction between substance and accident, then, is applicable to the entities of logic, as it is to artificial entities like tragedies.

At 23b33 he extends the interpretation of this notion of the contrary to negations of limits, showing on the same grounds that the contrary of 'the not good is not good' is that 'the not good is good.' He adds also that by this procedure, as well as the one that he previously used, it is shown that the contrary of 'the good is good' is 'the good is not good,' bringing his argument, so to speak, full circle.

Since all the examples given so far have been indefinite declarings, or those in which the predication is not made by virtue of a whole, 'human is human' rather than 'all humans are human,' and science exists by virtue of a whole and not through indefinite predications, this too must be incorporated into the interpretation. The contrary to what is by virtue of a whole must also be by virtue of a whole, as the contrary of 'all good is good' is 'no good is good. The reason, he says, is that if, in the opinion that 'the good is good,' one intends the good to be by virtue of a whole, that change does not change the predication. It might also be formulated as 'all that is good is good.'[24] And in addition, the same argument holds as well, as it did before, of the negation, what is not good.

In the final paragraph Aristotle completes the statement of contrariety that is essential for scientific predication. The problem of interpretation he says is that of expressing in vocal or written symbols the realities implicated in the soul.[25] The matters in the soul, of course are the forms of the realities in experience. In discussing the logical relations between opinions, we have been talking of matters concerning the soul. Affirmings and negatings are the written or vocal representations of these, as these are the representations of reality. Thus concerning the same thing, the contrary of the affirming by virtue of a whole is the negating by virtue of a whole, as 'the good is good' and 'all men are good,' or when the contrary entity is stated as 'nothing' or 'no one,' or when the contrary lies in the predication to make it a contradiction, 'not everything' or 'not everyone.' It is then apparent that whether we are speaking of opinions or their contraditions, the true is never contrary to the true, and the same must be true of the written and vocal symbols. For contraries are opposites and

24. The verbalization has been deliberately changed from that given in the translation to accommodate the latitude of the Greek.

25. The precision in this statement is crucial to grasp. It shows why the statement that the problem of interpretation is a problem about reality, or the determination of what reality is, or anything of that sort, is a serious misunderstanding. Such misunderstanding exists in the writings of some, like Walter Watson or David Dilworth, cited above, pp. 114 and 116, in the otherwise commendable attempt to proselytize the schema of Richard McKeon. But interpretation, as McKeon himself carefully shows, is not the problem of determining what reality is. It simply implicates a conception of reality when it is done. Interpretation, as Aristotle himself shows in this treatise, is the problem of reason's putting the limits or entities of discourse together in predications in such a manner as to be consonant with reality or what is.

truth is not opposed to truth. Many truths are stated of the same thing,[26] but simultaneously contraries are not.

With these two small treatises of his logic Aristotle has completed the statement of two of the three structures that must be imposed upon 'stating' in respect of its material parts, according with his procedure that is complete by virtue of using the most complete of causes. It therefore has the capacity, lacking in the others, to include, not only what the other procedures are capable of stating, but also what encompasses them.

The first problem in inquiry, is determining the sorts of entities which are the irreducible limits in the analysis of 'stating,' (as in the *Categories*). The second is determining the formation of the predicatings between such entities, in such manner as to make possible the correlation between any stating and the implicated reality, (as in *Concerning Interpretation*). This material side of logic has one more function, the manner in which a third entity, a cause, may be used to justify the predication of two others, as in the *Prior Analytics*. This is method and, like interpretation, establishes priorities in existence. For the being of the premises is the basis of the being of the conclusion. The material factor of logic thus involves entities (1) in their singularity, (2) in predicated pairs, or (3) in the linkage of three entities to make a syllogism. Having examined the first two in this book, we will examine the third in Vol. II.

Following this examination of the matter, the form of argumentation is fixed by the nature of the principles on which that argumentation depends. There are three forms of principle, the nature of things, accepted opinion, and what seems to be, examined respectively in the *Posterior Analytics*, the *Of Topics*, and *Concerning Sophistical Refutations*. These we will examine in Vols. III and IV of this series on Aristotle's logic.

26. This sentence at 24b8, here freely interpreted, is one of many, poorly articulated in Aristotle's rough archives, whose meaning is clear, though his expression is not.